Wishing you
an amazing
connection to
Spirit !! :)
♡ Motherella

MW00978323

UNVEIL YOUR INTUITION

A WORKBOOK CONNECTING YOU WITH YOUR HIGHER SELF AND SPIRIT GUIDANCE

Michelle "Motherella" Piper

BALBOA.PRESS

A DIVISION OF HAY HOUSE

Copyright © 2020 Michelle "Motherella" Piper.

All rights reserved. No part of this book may be used or reproduced by any means, graphic, electronic, or mechanical, including photocopying, recording, taping or by any information storage retrieval system without the written permission of the author except in the case of brief quotations embodied in critical articles and reviews.

Balboa Press books may be ordered through booksellers or by contacting:

Balboa Press
A Division of Hay House
1663 Liberty Drive
Bloomington, IN 47403
www.balboapress.com
1 (877) 407-4847

Because of the dynamic nature of the Internet, any web addresses or links contained in this book may have changed since publication and may no longer be valid. The views expressed in this work are solely those of the author and do not necessarily reflect the views of the publisher, and the publisher hereby disclaims any responsibility for them.

The author of this book does not dispense medical advice or prescribe the use of any technique as a form of treatment for physical, emotional, or medical problems without the advice of a physician, either directly or indirectly. The intent of the author is only to offer information of a general nature to help you in your quest for emotional and spiritual well-being. In the event you use any of the information in this book for yourself, which is your constitutional right, the author and the publisher assume no responsibility for your actions.

This workbook is for information purposes only. At no time is this workbook meant to be used as professional training. The Author has made sure that the information in this book was correct at the time of press. The information in this book is by no means professional medical advice, so the reader must consult a medical professional at that point. The Author does not assume and hereby disclaims the release of all liability to any party for any loss, damage, misuse, or free will caused by this book. The Author and distributors are not responsible for any adverse effects resulting from the use of the suggestions outlined in this workbook.

Any people depicted in stock imagery provided by Getty Images are models, and such images are being used for illustrative purposes only. Certain stock imagery © Getty Images.

Cover and interior design by
Claudio Mendrano
Sannicola Media Productions, Inc.
For more information, visit www.motherella.com
or email team@motherella.com

Print information available on the last page.

ISBN: 978-1-9822-4669-3 (sc)
ISBN: 978-1-9822-4670-9 (e)

Library of Congress Control Number: 2020907067

Balboa Press rev. date: 04/21/2020

CONTENTS

DEDICATION

I am indebted to my husband, children, and mom who have supported me throughout this entire journey and pushed me for success. There were a lot of highs and lows, but it was worth it. Also, thank you to the rest of my family and friends who have been right by my side along the way. I am grateful for all of you.

To my team: Claudio, Michelle, and Marni your love and support goes far beyond what I could have imagined. I appreciate you and all your hard work in making all my creations come to fruition.

To my Motherella Badasses who have been on this decades-long journey with me, I love you like family and strive to continue to share my gifts, knowledge, and wisdom with you and the world.

To my greatest teachers: The Divine, my Spirit Guides, and my ancestors. Thank you for showing me the way each day and training me to be the best authentic version of myself in this lifetime. I am committed to sharing your incredible information, messages, and stories from Beyond. My mission is to create a beautiful world full of love and kindness while helping people become their best authentic selves through connection.

I couldn't do all of this without all of you.

Much love, Motherella

INTRODUCTION

Mediumship has been part of my life since I can remember. My first encounter was when I was just six years old. A small girl appeared to me in my bedroom one evening. She informed me that she was my sister and that she had died through suffocation. *Yes, I met my sister, Lisa, in what I thought was a dream.* Prior to this evening, I didn't know I even had a sister. I was an only child, or so I thought. After this Sprit encounter, I immediately told my mother, who then validated my Spirit connection with my deceased sister. I often tell the detailed story at my live shows. Ever since that experience, I began seeing and hearing the departed and other Beings of the Afterlife quite frequently. I had moments where I would play with the Spirits. They became my "imaginary" friends. I was an odd child. I spent my "playtime" in dark spaces, cellars, attics, etc. My grandfather, who I inherited my "gifts" from, would frequently take me to the cemetery. These were some of my special memories that I will never forget. As I grew older, I became more and more aware of my abilities. At one point, I tried to shut my abilities off. When this didn't happen, I instead began ignoring them.

In my early 30s, despite my attempt to disconnect, my abilities had returned full swing, stronger, and even more profound. I became a student to the Spirit world, and Spirits became my teachers. I have never taken a class or course to evolve or develop my gift. It was instant for me and I learned through my experiences, channeling, Spirit Guides, Angels, loved ones, other dimensional Beings in the Universe, and now…my clients.

After 45 years of connecting with the Afterlife, I decided it was time to compile my learning into a workbook that can help others achieve the same foundation for connection. Years of my wisdom, teachings, experiences, and channeled learning have been placed into this workbook. My life path and purpose are to put as many lightworkers, healers, psychics, and mediums into this world. This will be my mission until my death from the human world. I have dedicated my life to this work. I have endured many challenges, setbacks, judgements and rock bottom moments throughout my career. However, because I possess profound faith in my Universe, nothing can steer me off.

I hope you enjoy this workbook. I wish you all a beautiful connection to your higher self, Spirit Guides, Angels, and loved ones. May this workbook shed new light on your inner power and authentic self. More importantly, my wish is that all of you live your best life now by becoming the true Badass you are meant to be in this lifetime. Keep depositing love and kindness into this world without judgement or anger. Together, and as a community, we can restore the beauty in this world as it was originally intended.

Much love,

Motherella

This workbook WAS NOT written to:

- Get a non-believer to believe.
- Combat your individual philosophies or belief systems.
- Argue your organized religion views and religious practice.
- Persuade you to stop conformed thinking based on how society dictates you to live.
- Connect you with negative energies, ghosts or other Spirits in the Afterlife.
- Call yourself anything professional such as a psychic medium just because you completed the activities in this workbook.

This workbook WAS written to:

- Unlock your soul through awareness and awakening.
- Unveil your intuition.
- Connect you with your higher self and Spirit.
- Understand the three levels of consciousness (3D, 4D and 5D).
- Understand the difference between ego and higher self.
- Understand the difference between Angels, Spirit Guides, Loved Ones, etc.
- Understand the difference between natural-born intuition, psychic gifts, and mediumship abilities.
- Unveil your own natural-born psychic mediumship gifts and abilities.

I do declare here that this workbook is not meant for anyone to elicit, disrupt, chastise, or randomly connect with the paranormal, supernatural, and Afterlife in anyway shape or form.

CHAPTER ONE

INTUITION

If you find yourself exploring the internet searching for the definition of *intuition*, you will find there is a slew of definitions and even theories about what intuition is and where intuition comes from.

For purposes of this workbook, I have provided you with my definition of **INTUITION**:

"Intuition is a non-conscious influence that emotionally moves through your body from your gut to your brain giving you an instinctual feeling or sensation. These feelings and sensations allow you to experience a deep soul connection with your higher self and your Higher Power (a.k.a. God, Source, Divine, etc.)"

Intuition is best described as a calm, impersonal feeling. Intuition is also referred to as gut feeling, inner voice, inner knowing, or sixth sense.

Clients often ask me, "How can I develop or tap into my own intuition?" My response is always this, "It isn't about tapping in; it is about awakening your soul and doing the inner work to evolve, grow, and enhance your natural-born gift of intuition."

We are all born with the gift of intuition. In my professional opinion, despite the claims out there written by various spiritual and metaphysical teachers, we are all natural-born psychics and mediums. Using your natural-born gifts of intuition, psychic skills, and mediumship abilities takes a long time to develop and strengthen. It takes continuous practice.

An intuitive, psychic, and medium are always in training and that training is for life. Your growth in these skills and abilities will never stop.

Did you know that intuition is equally present in everyone? Nothing separates it from you. You cannot escape your intuition, but you can turn it off, shut it down and ignore it. Intuition is generally turned off or shut down somewhere between your early childhood and young adult life. This is a result of your upbringing, along with many external factors such as:

- Being raised in a certain culture
- The way family morals are taught
- Being brought up in a conformed society
- Following organized religion views and religious practices
- Family embedded beliefs systems which creates limited thinking

Young children begin using their gift of intuition upon birth. As they grow older, that intuition is shut down or suppressed. This is because many children aren't raised in a spiritually intuitive family environment. Therefore, they aren't taught early on what intuition is, what it means, or how it works.

Some humans have a stronger intuition than others. Humans who possess a strong intuition allow themselves to live from a place of inner knowing and higher consciousness. I describe higher consciousness as this, *"a hard to reach mental state of a spiritually minded human that can connect with their true self and the spirit world outside of the human mind."* Those humans with a higher consciousness are strongly connected to their higher self and their Higher Power. I describe higher self as this, *"an eternal, conscious Being who is connected strongly to one's soul and one's real self."* Those humans with strong intuition can live and make decisions outside of human thinking and the subconscious ego. A strong intuitive, like myself, make their higher consciousness their way of life and are guided solely through their inner knowing (a.k.a. gut instinct).

Your intuition helps you dive into your creative self and fuels your inner power with an energy flow for your fulfillment and purpose. Your intuition opens yourself up to your higher consciousness within you and helps you work with your true guidance and inner knowing. Your intuition is also your innate ability to perceive real truth and solid inner knowing through trust, faith, higher self, and higher consciousness without logic, reasoning, or analysis.

Living through your intuition is a way of life. To fully experience solid intuition, you must learn to step out of your own way, avoid your shadows of self-doubt, repel uncertainty, rid lack of trust, and most importantly STOP your fear. You must consistently enter yourself into a mental state of clarity and confidence that cannot be deterred by any of your subconscious ego or external influences. It sounds hard to do but trust me, with practice, you can do it! Once you fully experience this connection as a way of life, you will want to live no other way.

"INTUITION IS YOUR OWN PERSONAL REFLECTION,
PERCEPTION, AND EXPERIENCE."
~ MOTHERELLA

TEST YOUR INTUITION

1. Do you often get a "strong" feeling about something, most often in your chest or stomach? If yes, describe how it feels. If no, why do you think you don't?

2. Do you ever have the feeling that something feels "off"? If yes, describe how it feels. If no, why do you think you don't?

3. Do you have this deep sensation, feeling or knowing but second-guess it and then it turns out you were correct? If yes, describe why you second-guessed it.

4. Do you evaluate your decisions based on "gut instinct"? If yes, describe how. If no, describe why not.

5. Do you instantly have an inner knowing or gut response when you meet people (a.k.a. vibe)? If yes, describe why and how that feeling presents itself. If no, why do you think you don't?

6. Do you immediately know when someone is lying to you? If yes, describe the feeling of how or why you know. If no, why do you think you can't tell?

If you answered yes to one or more of these questions, you are working with intuition. If no, you have some work to do!

WAYS TO SHARPEN YOUR INTUITION

1. Learn to quiet your mind.

2. Make silence your best friend.

3. Practice "feeling" things by using your senses instead of using your mind, especially when trying to make decisions.

4. Learn to let go of fear and worry.

5. Practice separating ego vs. higher self (more in the upcoming chapters).

6. Meditate and journal.

7. Work on trusting your gut through feeling.

Write what led you to this book in the space below:

At the end of this workbook, you will be asked to reflect on this writing prompt.

Write what three blocks you have when it comes to working with your intuition.

1.

2.

3.

Write three goals for developing your intuition.

1.

2.

3.

At the end of this workbook, you will be asked to reflect on this writing prompt.

CHAPTER TWO

LEVELS OF CONSCIOUSNESS

Your innate intuition can bring you to a higher level or frequency of expanded consciousness allowing you to connect with your Higher Power for true guidance. This can happen when you are working through your superconscious.

There are different energetic intensities at each level of your consciousness. Each level contributes to its own influences for you. The first step to developing your intuition is understanding the three levels of consciousness.

The three levels of consciousness are:

1. **Superconscious** = center, frontal lobe = higher self (5D)
2. **Conscious** = middle part of brain = rationalization (4D)
3. **Subconscious** = lower part of brain = ego/fear (3D)

Many people are unaware of what the 3D, 4D, and 5D dimensional realities are. You will hear many spiritual, metaphysical, and quantum physics teachers reference these dimensional realities. Some of these teachings can be very in-depth and overcomplicated for some people. Because there are various explanations, I am providing a basic understanding based on my own personal experiences and years of channeling my Spirit Guides.

The "D" stands for "dimensions". The numbers in front of the D stand for the dimensional levels. Those dimensional levels are not a physical place, but rather an energetic frequency and conscious vibration. Our world, as we speak, has been in a period of Ascension since 2012. The Ascension is not a physical place or someplace located out into the galaxy. Rather, the Ascension is an energetic shift for humans' spiritual awakening. This awakening is meant to move humans from a 3D low subconscious level to a higher frequency and vibration known as the 5D superconscious level. The Ascension process is much needed for this world and for all of us to live a better life. The Ascension process will help the world fill back up with love and kindness while being the caretakers of nature and humankind. Some spiritual, metaphysical, and quantum physics teachers may reference the Ascension as "The Shift". Many of you have heard me speak about this on my social media, courses, live videos, etc. We are in the height of it right now. To help you understand the conscious levels, I have placed the numerical Ds after each level of consciousness (see previous page).

It is in my professional opinion, that people who live in ego, low vibration, and the false realities (realist views, which I call spiritually asleep), live in a 3D reality with the lowest levels of conscious frequencies. People who live in a 4D reality are stuck between the 3D and 5D frequencies. Those people who live in 5D reality have profound faith, trust, Spirit connection, soul connection, abundance, and inner wealth. Those people are spiritually awake. With that said, let's look at the levels of consciousness a little more closely.

THE SUPERCONSCIOUS LEVEL:

The superconscious level is your true connection and communication between your higher self and Higher Power. Your Higher Power is remarkably individualized based on your belief system. My explanation of a Higher Power is, *"a supernatural Being, or supreme Being of power often referred to as God, Source, Divine, etc."* For the purposes of this workbook, I will also be referencing your Higher Power connection as the Divine.

The superconscious level is where your Divine true guidance lies. This is what many spiritual and metaphysical teachers refer to as, "The 5D". Your superconscious mind is solution-oriented. You too must be solution- oriented to draw forth your own guidance. How do you become solution- oriented? You start by asking your Divine.

Being able to divide and separate your conscious level from your subconscious level while still being able to unite them is your amazing superconscious at work. Strong intuition, deep inner knowing, and heightened clarity flows from this level of conscious expansion. Also, your superconscious is always working during the time between wakefulness and sleep. Because of this, you may tend to drift off and find yourself daydreaming frequently, or you may be a vivid dreamer at night.

When it comes to dreaming and any sort of intuitive development (including psychic mediumship), it is imperative not to analyze, overthink, or self-interpret your dreams. Dreams are a form of clairvoyance, which is a psychic mediumship ability called "clear seeing." Dreams are inaccurate ways of receiving your intuitive messages and Divine guidance. You cannot control your dreams.

In my courses and programs, I am always telling students, "do NOT try to interpret nor expand on your dreams while practicing, developing, or working with your intuition and higher consciousness expansion." This is because your interpretations can stem from your subconscious ego and not true Divine guidance, thereby creating unnecessary anxiety and energetic chaos coupled with false and inaccurate Divine guidance. Again, dreams cannot be controlled by you, so it is hard to rely on your dreams for intuitive guidance. If you are a reputable dream interpreter, awesome! However, if you want to learn more about dream interpretation, do so from a reliable source. While using this workbook, simply use your dreams as a reference instead of intuitive Divine guidance.

Here is an easy way to understand the basics for the three levels of your conscious mind:

Superconscious = unitive, sees all is whole = readily draws solutions so problems and solutions are viewed as one (5D).

Conscious mind = analytical = separate and distinct in everything (4D).

Subconscious mind = intrusive = trickster = relies on past impressions, thoughts, feelings, and embedded beliefs (3D).

Most humans are asleep at the subconscious level. When humans are asleep at this level, they live their life like a realist. A realist, by definition, is a person who accepts life or a situation as it is; they see that life and situation are accurate and true to life. For the purposes of this workbook, I will be referring to these two states of being as spiritually asleep and spiritually awake.

A spiritually asleep human sees their world as reality. A spiritually awake human sees their world as non-reality. Asleep humans get caught up in a belief system that "what appears in front of them is their real truth." These humans live solely in the subconscious, or between the subconscious and conscious levels (3D and 4D). Rarely, if at all, do they access their superconscious because they don't allow themselves to live past their immediate existence. This level of thinking is consumed by fear and worry which paralyzes them. This way of thinking also makes it difficult for them to step into their inner power and live their true authentic self. Spiritually asleep humans constantly need proof and validity for everything of their existence. Their world is validated by external existence rather than internal being.

Here are some examples of a spiritually asleep human vs. spiritually awake human:

Spiritually Asleep humans believe:

- hard work = good pay = a good living.
- money in their bank account = success.
- success = is a title or status = material goods = good job with a high salary.
- work as hard as possible for retirement.

Spiritually Awake humans believe:

- enjoying what you love = living your soul path and purpose = a fulfilled life with financial freedom.
- money is energy = a bank account doesn't define them = the Universe provides unlimited amounts of wealth.
- success = inner wealth = inner wealth mirrors and matches outer wealth = success comes from within.
- love, life path, soul purpose, soul freedom, abundance, and fulfillment.

Spiritually asleep humans live outside of their intuition and superconscious. They have conformed or limited thinking. Spiritually asleep humans have no inner knowing or spiritual connection whatsoever. And, no, you cannot live between the two ways of life as an intuitive. Spiritually asleep humans seek guidance externally, have trust issues, and are often up against setbacks or blocks. They end up on the wrong path and live very unfulfilled life. Because of this, the asleep human will never become their best, true, and authentic version of themselves unless they decide to make the conscious shift. They will always be on a quest for physical evidence and facts to guide them through life. Even worse, they will live their life around what others see for them or the way society dictates for them. Unless they can break through this thinking and expand their consciousness, they will never truly be living for themselves.

Spiritually awake humans live through their superconscious level, possess a strong inner knowing, and intuitively know that nothing outside of the soul exists. Again, their outer world is not "reality." They live vibrationally high and have an untouchable faith that the Divine has everything worked out for them. They know they have limitless potential and that the human world is limitless. They live without fear and worry and need nothing to validate their inner knowing except their signs from the Divine. Their soul is awake and alive.

As stated earlier, spiritually asleep humans live between the conscious and subconscious level. This 3D level of thinking is where people believe everything they are told. Therefore, it's hard for them to think for themselves from their own intuition. Let us look further into these two levels (refer back to previous pages for the superconscious level).

THE CONSCIOUS LEVEL:

The conscious level is your rational state that helps guide you in your day to day life. This level is using your senses and analyzation for decision making. This level is where your decisions can be strongly affected by others and the outside world. This level of consciousness is problem- oriented. Because of this, it is difficult to make decisions or have solid certainty because the analytic mind sees all the possibilities and solutions. However, the conscious level can help you decide which one is best. Because of all the back and forth at this level, you tend to feel unsure, uncertain and undecided. This is what many spiritual and metaphysical teachers refer to as, "The 4D" reality.

THE SUBCONSCIOUS LEVEL:

The subconscious level is your weak, dream-like state that is unrestricted and where your ideas flow. This part of the conscious mind is the storage area for deep rooted, embedded impressions and imprints from your past lives and past trauma. When working through your past lives, this level of consciousness needs the most inner work to uproot and re-write old imprinted and embedded thoughts. This level of the mind determines your current patterns and behavior. When you dream, you are using your subconscious mind. This is why I stated earlier, "do not trust your dreams." The subconscious mind can trick you into thinking you are receiving intuitive guidance when instead you are using past impressions, false beliefs, and ego. This level of the mind keeps us in a constant state of fear, worry, lack, suppression, and unfulfillment. This is what many spiritual and metaphysical teachers refer to as, "The 3D" reality.

At this point, your mind might already be wandering, "Wow, this sounds like me." Do not fret my dear, I got you! Learning to control your state of consciousness takes time, patience, and practice. Just know you can do it! You can choose which level of your consciousness you want to expand on and work with it a little each day.

The fastest and quickest way to control your consciousness and expand it at the same time is through meditation. Meditation is a practice that trains your mind to be still, calm, and clear in an emotionally stable state of being. This practice expands your higher consciousness and connects you with your higher self. With practice, consistency, and time, meditation will help you gain control over your mind, feelings, and emotions. Mind control is a practice, an inner being, and a way of life.

To strengthen your intuitive ability, you must learn to meditate, and you must meditate daily. Not everyone meditates the same way and most definitely not everyone needs to meditate lying down with their eyes closed. I teach my students to do what I call, "awake state meditation", where the student practices various meditative homework prompts while awake. My explanation of "awake state meditation" is, *"learning the ability to calm, quiet, and still the mind while doing relaxing and calming activities such as walking outdoors, journal writing, driving in car, house cleaning, etc."*

If you are looking to work with your intuition, expand into your superconscious, and receive Divine guidance – then journal writing alongside meditation is a must. These two tools, when combined, are very powerful sources when connecting with your higher self and your Divine guidance.

"TRUE GUIDANCE TAKES YOU INSIDE YOURSELF, NOT OUTSIDE. OUTSIDE GUIDANCE IS FALSE GUIDANCE."
~ MOTHERELLA

TEST YOUR CONSCIOUSNESS

1. Do you live with constant fear or worry? If yes, write why you feel you do.

2. Do you trust that everything will work out for you in the end without you controlling it? If no, write why.

3. Do you find that your ideas, dreams and desires are easily manifested into your reality? If no, with everything you just read, where could your block be to be living the life you truly desire?

4. Are you one to say any of the following terms: "Proof is in the pudding" or "I will believe it when I see it"? If yes, based on everything you just read, do you feel your mindset is blocking you in your human reality? Write how.

Ask yourself the following ten questions and answer yes or no:

1. Do you try to control the outcome of everything?

2. Do you try to control everything and everyone?

3. Do you trust your Universe enough to let go and let the Divine handle it?

4. Do you feel you are living your true authentic self?

5. Do you feel you are on your path and purpose?

6. Do you feel you are meant for more, but cannot seem to get there?

7. Do you constantly live in fear or worry?

8. Do you overthink?

9. Does your mind often spiral out of control?

10. Do you honestly feel you are happy and fulfilled?

Take a moment and reflect on the previous answers that tested your consciousness. When done, answer the following questions:

1. Are you spiritually asleep or spiritually awake? Why?

2. What three steps are you willing to take this month to work towards your superconscious expansion and connection with your higher self?

3. What are three goals you will make to shift your limited beliefs, limited thinking or false truths in order to expand into working with your own intuition, higher self, superconscious and Divine guidance?

WAYS TO HELP MIND CONTROL

1. Meditation.
2. Journal writing.
3. Breath work.
4. Listen to your thoughts and acknowledge them, but don't react, respond or engage until you have been able to separate ego from guidance.
5. Self-talk.
6. Make peace with your mind.
7. Detach from the thoughts themselves and realize that thoughts are just simply thoughts, not absolutes.
8. Observe and explore your mind through journal writing.
9. Re-train your mind through past life regression therapy or inner soul work re-writing.
10. Practice self-love and self-care. Be gentle and patient with yourself.

From the list above, choose three ways you will practice your mind control over the next month and write "how" below. For example: I will wait from a negative triggered thought to form and immediately stop myself and turn that thought into a positive and the minute I begin to feel anxious, I will stop right away and begin doing breath work.

AWAKE STATE MEDITATION EXERCISE

1. Pick a place to walk in nature either around water, a park, walking trail, etc. (I don't recommend within a busy neighborhood because of traffic, people, distractions, etc.)
2. Still and silence the mind. You may carry you cell phone, however, you will not listen to music nor use your cell phone during this time.
3. This is a slow, leisure walk, pace yourself.
4. Use your senses: take in the sounds around you, the smells, the feeling of your breath going in and out, and feel the sun or air on your face.
5. Slowly inhale and exhale. Let that amazing air fill your lungs.
6. Get connected to your inner body. Feel your breath moving, your blood flowing, your bones shifting.
7. Have gratitude for being alive and well.
8. Your affirmation is: *"I am alive. I am well. I have freedom to enjoy life."*
9. Now, you will connect by stating the following: *"Hello Spirit Guides and Angels. Show me what I need to know. Fill my thoughts with guidance and what is it that I need to know today. Thank you."*
10. When completing your walk, go home and journal ALL that you felt, saw, and heard on the blank page provided.

MY AWAKE STATE MEDITATION EXPERIENCE

Write your reflection below.

CHAPTER THREE

PAST LIVES

Every human has lived at least ONE past life. Many humans, like myself, have lived multiple past lives. Did you know that your one or more past lives can be dictating your NOW, as well as your future?

When unveiling your intuition and working through conscious expansion, it is great to simultaneously work through some of your past life imprints. How can you live your true authentic self or embark on your path and purpose when your past is holding you back?

Your consciousness can live pre-existing because of your previous life information and encoding. In other words, your present is an extension of your past. The reason why this workbook is helpful, not only for your current life and consciousness, it can also help you relate, become aware, and identify with your past life which is contributing to your current self-sabotage and blocks. We all have karma debt that is brought into our current human existence. Part of learning to unveil your intuition, expanding your levels of consciousness, connecting with your higher self, and connecting with your Spirit Guides is to unravel, decode, and re-write the past. Pay your karma debt.

This workbook is only bringing you the basic information of past lives, because to understand, learn, and work through your past life imprints, codes, contracts, and karma debt it would take another whole book. It is also important to briefly discuss because while you are going through the unveiling process, you may start to receive some past life memories.

Your eternal consciousness has been imprinted and encoded with stored information, data, and emotional energy from your past lives. All that is influencing you right now and will continue to re-surface during the unveiling. This is all part of spiritual awakening process and evolving your soul.

You may experience:

- Dreams from other lifetime (i.e. such as seeing yourself in other countries and eras)
- Déjà vu: A sense of familiarity, like you have been there or done that before
- Increased awareness of self-sabotage or self-destructive behaviors (such as attracting toxic relationships, addiction, etc.)
- Phobias
- Fearing death and chronic worry of injury or death

I want to point out that karma is NOT punishment. Karma is basically a mirrored reflection of our energy that we are putting out to the Universe and boomerangs back us as a transformed learned lesson. Karma allows us to learn lessons to evolve and grow as a soul, but also to experience love.

I have performed many past life readings for clients. It takes a lot of work and time to dig deep into your past life. Though a psychic medium can access these past lives or even access your Akashic Records, you will never be able to get to the root of past life issues, nor work on these issues in just one reading. Trust me, it won't work.

Your Akashic Records is a vital record of all you are as a soul: past, present, and future. This vibrational record is available for every human soul to access. Every soul has their own record recorded. These Akashic

Records, which I call, Your Soul's Divine Library, is a dimension of consciousness that has all that your soul has ever experienced, thought, felt, or done in its existence from your past, present, and your future possibilities.

A skilled and trained professional such as a psychic medium, healer, past life regression practitioner, and an Akashic Records reader, is the best way to begin guiding you to access your soul records. Once you have access, you will want to work hard a doing the inner work. Many spiritual teachers call this Past Life Regression work.

Past life regression work is done through meditation and hypnosis to uncover your memories from you past life incarnations. This is also a great technique and tool to access your Akashic Records. When done correctly, you can really catapult your inner healing and mend the past that haunts you. Past life regression work takes a lot of inner work on the individual's part. A big part of this work is helping you with your Soul Contracts.

SOUL CONTRACT:

A soul contract are the agreements your soul has made prior to being born. That contract is brought with on your incarnation. We can also have these contract agreements with other souls, who we meet throughout our soul journey. These contracts are what teaches us our lessons in our current lifetime.

Because of these contracts, many of my clients and students often hear me say, "Be careful when you are manifesting a soul mate vs. a life partnership." A soulmate contract can be made with multiple souls. Do you keep attracting in the same type of relationships? If yes, then you haven't learned the lesson from that soul contract. So instead, you keep manifesting in the same crap over and over again. Learn the lesson peeps!

As I tell my clients, soulmates come into our lives with a deep connection and an instant pull. Most of the time we are thinking, "I have never felt like this before." Then suddenly, as things are moving along, they are whisked out of our lives in thin air. You are left dumbfounded and bewildered. Well, this is because they were a soulmate contract.

When manifesting love, be sure you are asking the Universe to align you with a life partnership rather than asking for your soulmate. If you are asking for your soulmate, trust me, you are getting your prayers answered in multiple ways and multiple times. Soulmates can be mentors, teachers, parents, siblings, friends, animals, AND love interests. Therefore, be careful how you're asking the Universe for love.

As said earlier, a skilled and trained professional such as a psychic medium, healer, past life regression practitioner, and an Akashic Records reader will help you break the soul contracts you have made before your incarnation to stop the madness, heal from within, and be able to live a life of love, happiness, and abundance. Working with your soul contract will help you:

- Cut your past energetic cords.
- Stopping your karmic patterns, blocks, and self-sabotage.
- Pay your karmic debt in full.
- Break all soul contracts in this lifetime.

For the purposes of this workbook, it is important to recognize patterns that keep occurring and identify if you are blocking your innate intuition during them. There are various ways to reflect, remember, resonate, and connect with your past life in your stored memory of your subconscious.

People with previous life blocks:

- Don't dream
- Have little to no visions
- Feel tense, scared or worried about enhancing their gifted intuition
- Experience anxiety about psychic mediumship or that the Divine is going to punish them
- They saw Angels as a child and this diminished as they got older
- Feel highly sensitive
- Chronically worry about what family, friends or others think

How to heal blocks:

- Set boundaries with people
- Support with like-minded souls
- Cut cords
- Ritual work
- Past Life Regression
- Positive affirmations/mantras
- Meditation
- Healings
- Crystals
- Lifestyle improvements
- Asking for help from the Divine and Angels

TESTING YOUR PAST LIFE MEMORY

1. Have you ever met someone you had an instant connection with? Write who that person was and how it felt.

2. Have you ever met someone who you felt you knew before? Write who that person was and how it felt.

3. Have you ever had an immediate attraction (sexual, or intimate) with someone? Write who that person was and how it felt.

4. Have you ever visited a place or been somewhere that you felt you have been before, even though you have not? Write where and describe it.

5. Do you have a natural talent that comes to you very easily (i.e. writing, music, singing, sports, etc.)? If yes, describe it in detail.

6. If you have children, do you have a very deep connection with them or with one of your children that you cannot explain? If no children, maybe a niece, nephew, cousin, etc. Write who that person is and how it feels.

7. Do you feel you are more of a parent in your relationships than a spouse/partner? If yes, describe how it feels.

8. Do you keep attracting in the same thing over and over into your life (i.e. debt, job issues, relationship dysfunction, etc.) Write what you keep attracting in and how.

9. Do you keep failing at romantic relationships? Write how.

10. Do you have addictions or have an addictive personality (i.e. food, love interests, medication, drugs, risk taking behaviors, or anything unhealthy)? Write the addiction(s) and how.

11. Do you constantly fear illness and/or health issues and chronically talk about your health as if everything is related to a disease? Write how.

Take a moment and reflect on the above answers. Write a letter to yourself describing the lessons you have learned about yourself in this exercise.

MY PAST LIFE LESSONS I NOW RECOGNIZE ABOUT MYSELF
Write your lessons letter to yourself here.

SOUL CONTRACT RELEASE

This is a very basic soul contract release for you to try. This release should be performed on the next Full Moon. You are to read it aloud, outdoors, and sign the bottom with your name and date.

To my Divine, Spirit Guides, Angels, and Universal Beings,

I understand that, my soul agreed to this karmic contractual experience in this lifetime. This might include working hard for little or no happiness, love, money, health, and overall abundance. I refuse anything that does not serve me in this lifetime. As of now, I release all karmic debts and complete all soul contracts from my soul's agreement. These contracts are now and forevermore completed and forgiven.

To all my Universal Beings, Angels, and Spirit Guides that guide me, watch over me, and protect me, I deny karmic cords or connections to my family lineage, past lives, and other soul contracts. These have also been completed regarding their karmic debt of lack, self-sabotage, pain, and suffering.

From the beginning of my birth to the end of my soul's existence, I am now and forevermore freed and released of any karmic debt, blocks, fears, negativity, limiting beliefs, patterns, cords, and agreements of my soul contract. I release all physically, mentally, emotionally and spiritually non-supporting people and situations for my soul's path and purpose. All is dissolved at Divine speed, remembering the timing here on Earth.

I am now set free to move forward in my life with great love, health, wealth, happiness, and abundance. I deserve a rewarding life experience because it is my birthright. From this moment forward, I attract in all that I am worthy of for my abundant life.

Thank you. I love you all.

Name:_____ Date:_____

CHAPTER FOUR

CHAKRA BASICS

Yoga science teaches us that we have three bodies: the physical, the astral "energy" and the pure thought. Though this chapter isn't going full into depth with information about our Chakra system, it is important to understand the basics of our Chakra system to work effectively with your intuition, higher self and superconscious expansion.

In the ancient language, Sanskrit, Chakra means "wheel". The astral body has seven energy centers known as our chakra system, aka Sanskrit. These energy centers govern our various emotional and mental states. To even begin to understand your own Chakra system, you must first start with the inner knowing that you are an energy being of light, love, and wisdom. All humans are born with unlimited energy. You come into this human experience with energy and remarkable inner gifts and talents. These gifts and talents are your birthright. Becoming aware of your true authentic self and working in this human world with your natural-born gifts are part of your path and purpose for this current soul incarnation.

Your Chakra system, again, is energy. Your thoughts are energy. With that said, to keep your Chakra system clear, moving, and balanced, your thoughts and mind control must fuel your Chakra system's energy flow. Your thoughts determine how you act, feel, and what you attract into your human experience. Different energy centers, known as Chakras, that are in and around you, are affected by these thoughts and feelings.

The best way I describe these energy centers are like having badass rims on a luxury car. Now, imagine something like a tree branch or mop handle getting stuck in these rims when moving. Wham! The tire would stop, break, and wouldn't be able to turn or move when driving. Well, your Chakra system works the same way.

Negative thoughts and limited beliefs = the tree branch or mop handle that stops flow.

Though our body is comprised of many energy centers, your focus should be on the seven main Chakras for healing. These Chakra centers are your push of vital life force energy (a.k.a. ki, chi, or prana). Your Chakra system radiates and receives energy constantly. Each Chakra is energetically connected to your hormones, glands, and organs. Each Chakra has a strong influence on many areas of your life such as money, love, health, relationships, career, appetite, goals, aspirations, etc.

Again, for the purposes of this workbook, I won't be going into depth or further learning of your Chakra systems, that would take an entirely separate book. However, working with your intuition, higher self, and higher power connection, you must have a basic understanding of yourself as an energy being and that your Chakra system play a significant part of your intuition.

There are many resources available that discuss the Chakra system at length. I recommend accessing some of these resources as an adjunct to your intuitive development. Meditation is, again, the number one way to keep your Chakra system cleared, opened, and balanced. There are many Chakra meditations available for free on YouTube.

CHAKRA BLOCK CHECKLIST

Here are some signs and symptoms of a blocked Chakra system (There are many; I am just providing a few common ones I work with in my practice).

Circle each of the signs and symptoms that you relate to. If you circle more than two, you may want to perform a Chakra meditation (free on YouTube), receive a Chakra balancing or energy healing session from a reputable practitioner.

Circle all that apply:

Poor intuition

Inability to sleep or staying asleep

Headaches

Low vibration/depression

Constipation

Fatigue

Mood swings

Imbalanced

Thyroid issues

Blood pressure issues

Poor digestion/stomach issues

Infertility

Low sex drive

Fear/worry

Low self-esteem

Lack of confidence

Trust issues

Lack of willpower

Addiction or addictive behavior

Negative thinking

Review all the signs and symptoms you circled and state the following energetic releasing statement:

"I now wholeheartedly and effortlessly release all signs and symptoms that are blocking my mental, emotional, physical, and spiritual energy within my Chakra system.

My mind is with clarity. My energy is free.

I release all negative, toxic, and blocked energy now. I am mentally, emotionally, physically, and spiritually free.

I am in perfect balance."

QUICK CHAKRA CLEARING MEDITATION EXERCISE

I recommend doing this quick Chakra Clearing Meditation exercise as you work through this workbook. You may use longer meditations if you desire. However, if you are looking for a quick way to balance each day, then I recommend this. I do this each morning during my outdoor walk. This exercise can be performed when taking a shower, a bath, on a leisure walk, while drinking coffee, or right before reading this workbook.

1. Sit, walk, or stand in a place when you can quiet your mind.
2. Remove all external distractions.
3. Take six deep breaths and feel your breath as you are inhaling and exhaling.
4. Visualize a bright, diamond-white light surrounding you like a cylinder and encapsulating you in it.
5. Feel this bright, diamond-white light also flowing through your inner body with every breath from the top of your head to the bottom of your feet.
6. Take a huge deep breath, and visualize exhaling all negativity, toxicity, or blockages from your energy centers of your Chakra system.
7. Take an additional, slow and rhythmic six breaths.
8. Visualize the bright, diamond-white light cylinder being lifted above you and dissolving out into the Universe.

CHAPTER FIVE

CONNECTION TERMS

Before we dive into intuitive connection, you must first understand a few terms used in relation to intuitive connection. With an enormous amount of available spiritual and metaphysical literature, books, social media, teachings, etc. many common terms and their usage can get rather confusing and/or be interchanged inappropriately.

Below are some basic meanings behind these terms. These terms, once understood, will really help catapult your intuitive development in order to work more closely with your soul, spirit, ego, higher self, gut instinct, and Higher Power.

SOUL:

A soul is the spiritual essence of you. Your soul makes you who you are. Souls are immortal. Your soul is a distinct Spirit that is separate from the human physical body. Your soul is aware of your oneness with your Higher Power (i.e. God, Divine, Source, Buddha, etc.) Your soul evolves, grows, and develops in this life experience through higher self, expanded consciousness, and your Higher Power.

SPIRIT:

Spirit has two different definitions, yet, can blend into the same meaning. Your Spirit is your "I AM" and your awareness, along with knowing that you are one with the Divine, God, Source, etc. Spirit is also referred to as the energy Beings or Entities located in our galaxy, dimension, sky, Afterlife, and Universe. Both definitions are nonphysical, essences of energy. A Spirit is still a Being, just in another energetic dimensional space.

EGO:

Ego is your nagging voice shouting from your subconscious mind. Your ego is always talking you out of your desires and is a huge block for connecting with your higher self and Higher Power. Ego feeds and thrives off fear and worry. Your ego also stores everything from your past, especially negative trauma. The ego embeds these thoughts, feelings and emotions as imprints and mythical beliefs. Because of this, your ego has a huge effect on connecting with your higher self and living your true authentic version of you.

HIGHER SELF:

Your higher self (i.e. superconscious, gut, guidance) simply put is, "One with your true authentic self." Your higher self represents the best parts of you in your purest form. Your higher self can guide you when asking questions to help lead you on your chosen path.

SIGNS:

Signs are mysterious workings of the Universe that come in the physical form repeatedly through many things such as:

- Numbers: license plates numbers, addresses, receipts, clocks, and triplet numbers (i.e. 111, 333, 444).

- Deceased love one's anniversary, death, or birthday showing in the same format.
- Nature: animals or birds (i.e. cardinals, hawks, butterflies, wolves, dragonflies, etc.)
- Finding random coins or money (i.e. pennies, dimes, dollar bills)
- Words on a billboard or names on a commercial
- Sentences that people say
- Songs on the radio
- Smells or aroma (i.e. perfume, flowers, cigars, etc.)
- Electronics events (i.e. TV static, or music turning on and off)
- Lights flickering on and off
- Feeling a presence

Many times, people mistake signs for coincidences. In truth, there are no coincidences unless you are spiritually asleep. When you are on your right path, ask the Universe a question, need validation, or simply ask for a sign – the Universe provides it. Signs are the Universe's way of saying "pay attention." However, you are not to overthink your signs, nor over interpret them. In fact, sometimes, you aren't even meant to know the meaning behind them, but rather just acknowledge the signs and say "thank you" to the Universe. Signs are not only from loved ones who have passed, signs come from our Angels and Spirit Guides too.

ORBS:

Orbs are another big sign coming from the Spirit world. In my opinion, being able to capture an orb on video or pictures is the true experience of seeing a soul. Orbs are often caught on video or captured in pictures which can often be seen on many paranormal shows. Some paranormal writers and investigators who have photographed orbs have said that orbs have various colors. From some of the research I have done, an orb color represents different meanings. For me, an orb is the reflection of a soul. I believe each orb meaning is a departed soul, Spirit Guide, Angel, or dimensional Being.

The world is fascinated with paranormal shows that provide tangible proof that the Spirit world exists. As a psychic medium, it is only natural to be able to see or capture orbs. I will say this, our newest technology of smart phones has people thinking they see orbs when taking photos when in fact the spheres are just sunlight or light reflections. Here is a clue: orbs will not follow you around, so if you see a green light following you while taking a photo with your smart phone, that is a reflective spot. An orb is fast and can be captured while moving in one direction or floating. It will not follow you around and it will not remain stationary.

SYNCHRONICITY/SYNCHRONIZED EVENTS:

This term is often confused with coincidence. Synchronicity or synchronized events are a human experience of two or more occurrences that occur after a thought, feeling, or statement and they occur at random or by chance.

GUT INSTINCT:

A natural-born, gift of intuition that presents itself as a strong feeling or inner knowing. This intuitive knowing is without logic, reason and rationale. Gut instinct is purely an intuitive emotional response sometimes felt in the pit of your stomach instead of a thought in your mind. This response is immediate with a strong understanding or knowledge of something. Yes, it is a feeling and yes, you "just know."

"MOST PEOPLE KNOW THE TRUE ANSWER IN THEIR GUT, BUT THEY TEND TO IGNORE THE RED FLAGS."
~ MOTHERELLA

TEST YOURSELF

Let's test your memory of terms below. Circle True or false:

1. Your soul is the spiritual essence of you.
   True | False
2. Your soul is part of your human physical body.
   True | False
3. Your Spirit means you are separate from your Higher Power (i.e. God, Source, Divine, etc.)
   True | False
4. A Spirit is an energy Being or Entity in our galaxy, dimension, sky, Afterlife, and Universe.
   True | False
5. A Spirit is still a Being, just in another energetic dimensional space.
   True | False
6. Your ego is the voice you should always be listening to.
   True | False
7. Your ego is the best way to connect with your higher self and Higher Power.
   True | False
8. Your ego stores everything from your past, is the basis for fear/worry, and can create blocks to your connection with your higher self and Higher Power.
   True | False
9. Your higher self can help lead and guide you on your path and purpose.
   True | False
10. Signs are superstitions and coincidences.
    True | False
11. Signs from the Universe come to us in the physical form when we need to pay attention or when we are on our right path.
    True | False
12. Synchronicities are two or more occurrences by random or chance.
    True | False
13. Gut instinct is a human skill that is learned and developed.
    True | False

ANSWER KEY IS ON THE NEXT PAGE.

ANSWER KEY:

1. T

2. F

3. F

4. T

5. T

6. F

7. F

8. T

9. T

10. F

11. T

12. T

13. F

Now that you understand these terms, let's talk more about connecting with your intuition through intuitive automatic writing.

CHAPTER SIX

CONNECTING TO SPIRIT THROUGH INTUITIVE AUTOMATIC WRITING

To receive clear and accurate guidance while connecting, you must:

- Believe and/or have profound faith
- Remove all doubt
- Trust yourself

Not all answers of intuitive guidance will come clearly to you every time. You can sometimes feel stuck or confused with the guidance you are receiving. Even so, the guidance you are receiving may seem unclear. When this happens, remain calm, be patient, and give it time.

Here are some steps to take when guidance seems unclear:

- Take a break from asking for answers
- Wait for the answers to flow over time
- Do not force the answers to you
- Release control of how or when you are getting the answers

Your intuitive guidance is received from your "Spirit Guides." Spirit Guides are assigned to you at birth once your soul's decision is made to come back to live your human life experience. Spirit Guides are your number one go-to for spiritual guidance. Your Spirit Guides have all your guidance for lessons to be learned, soul path, and life purpose.

They are big contributors when asking yourself...
"What is in store for my future?"
"How can I make the right decision?"
"When will I find love?"
"What is my purpose?"

Spirit Guides are your most accurate and clear forms of communication as an intuitive, and even more important as a psychic medium. When I am giving a psychic reading, which is different than a mediumship reading, my direct channel of guidance and information is coming from my Spirit Guides communicating with your Spirit Guides. Later in this workbook, I will be discussing the difference between psychics and mediums.

Your departed loved ones are not an integral part of your path and purpose. Your departed loved ones are Beings who have left the human experience and now exist in another energetic dimension. They are your continued love and protection in the Afterlife. Though they can be our "guardians" in the Afterlife when called upon, they aren't able to intervene with your soul path and purpose.

I cannot stress enough here: the best ways to connect with your guidance from Spirit Guides, connect to your loved ones, and develop a strong intuition is to get into the daily habit of meditating and journal writing. For over a decade, I have taught many workshops and courses on Intuitive Automatic Writing and how important it is to use as a psychic medium. Intuitive automatic writing allows your intuition to flow through you onto paper and access intuitive spiritual guidance from your Spirit Guides.

Intuitive automatic writing can be done by anyone who has a pen and paper and is willing to unveil their intuition and connect with their guidance. In addition, intuitive automatic writing has different levels of expertise. In fact, this skill is an advanced psychic mediumship skill used in many psychic mediumship practices. This advanced skill allows the psychic to channel information from a supernatural source, Spirit, and Afterlife. For the purposes of this workbook, we are only focusing on the basic intuitive automatic writing skill.

The intuitive automatic writing technique works with your higher self while connecting you with your Spirit Guides. You can dig deep into your soul's desire, while connecting with your higher self. Your higher self is also referenced in many teachings as "I AM." You will learn your true authentic self and soul identity through intuitive automatic writing.

When you begin to perform intuitive automatic writing, your guidance via Spirit Guide messages will flow through you automatically onto paper. This form of writing will help you gain insight, guidance, and validation. There is no control in your writing. If you are controlling the answers, then that is not intuitive guidance, that is ego writing.

Intuitive writing is also known as automatic or channeled writing. There are numerous authors and spiritual teachers that teach this technique from different perspectives. In this workbook, I will be discussing and teaching my form of intuitive connection that I myself practice and have taught for over a decade. My teachings have allowed many fellow students to achieve great connection results and many have gone on to practice this skill in their daily life, to work through healing, to connect with loved ones after grief, and even to use in a professional psychic mediumship or healing setting.

One of the incredible results of intuitive automatic writing is that you will learn to let your ego fall to the wayside while connecting with your higher self and connection. Because intuitive writing works all on its own, you will become a master at silencing your mind through this skill.

You may find many myths in your online research that intuitive automatic writing connects you with negative or evil Spirits and Entities. Many of these myths go on to state that these Spirits and Entities will take over your body and pen when writing.

Anyone who has had an in-person reading, attended my workshops, or has been in the audience at one of my shows have witnessed first-hand my intuitive automatic writing right before their very eyes. Last I checked, I am not possessed nor evil. Don't let modern day society with limited thinking and ego-driven guidance deter you from unveiling your intuition and spiritual connection. I have been writing messages from the Spirit world since I was very young. I have channeled hundreds of thousands of departed loved ones with written messages. I have never had a Whoopi Goldberg phenomenon like in the movie "Ghost", lol.

Now, let me be clear, can you get false messages through intuitive automatic writing? Yes, you can! However, that is only because you are writing with control and from ego rather than through your higher self and superconscious connection. Again, this is a skill that takes patience and practice.

With intuitive automatic writing, you are writing from your direct connection through your higher self and through your Spirit Guides. Therefore, that makes it impossible to connect with anything other than your higher self, Spirit Guides or ego.

Intuitive automatic writing will help you learn to quickly connect with your Spirit Guides, receive messages of guidance, explore your soul, gain answers to lessons that need to be learned in this lifetime, and break hindering patterns and blocks that anchor you down. I need to mention, that as an avid journal writer and teacher of this technique, journal writing is very different than intuitive automatic writing.

Intuitive automatic writing:

- Enhances your spiritual connection and intuitive abilities.
- Helps you work with your own soul and heart's desires.
- Empowers and motivates you through life.
- Allows you to flow with your Universe and spiritual guidance for your highest good.
- Will make you feel more grounded, clear, focused, and centered in life.
- Will provide you the tools to be able to set strong boundaries in your life.
- Provides you with higher wisdom and knowledge.
- Allows you to live your best version of you by working through your higher self as "I AM."

Committing to this practice allows you to almost instantly write down everything you are thinking, feeling or visualizing when flowing with your guidance. You will also begin to reveal and uncover things about yourself that you never could have imagined. Your true self and your life story will begin to shine through. You will be able to log your own timeline of events and signs. You will have validation and proof of your progress. Your written entries are a great reflection on evolvement, growth, and development overtime. I recommend that your intuitive automatic writing journal be a "sacred" one that is solely used for your intuitive development. You will not want to convolute these journal entries with other writings such as a gratitude journal or a journal for freewriting.

If you feel you don't like to write or don't have the time, then I can assure you, it will take you longer to develop, evolve, grow, develop, and unveil your intuition. It will take you longer to see yourself as a soul. It will take you longer to make your self-discovery to make massive changes in your life. It will take you longer to learn your past life lessons and current lessons in this lifetime. It will take you longer to develop a strong intuition and receive your own guidance daily.

MOTHERELLA'S 3 TO 5 SECOND RULE

ANYTHING THAT POPS UP IN YOUR HEAD WITHIN 3 TO 5 SECONDS IS ACCURATE GUIDANCE.

DON'T OVERTHINK IT.

DON'T SECOND GUESS IT.

~ Motherella

INTUITIVE AUTOMATIC WRITING

Answer the following questions with the FIRST thing that pops in your head. Don't overthink it, just let the answers flow…

1. If you had to tell your younger self something major you learned about yourself in your adult life, what would it be?

2. If you got to choose one thing you were passionate about as a child for your path and purpose, what would that be?

3. What does your "future self" look like with regards to your passion, path, and purpose?

INTUITIVE AUTOMATIC WRITING

Answer the following questions by letting the answers
flow through you in thought, feeling, vision, etc. Don't
second guess it or overthink your responses.

1. How many Spirit Guides do you have? (write the first number that
   pops in your head)

2. Try to connect with ONE Spirit Guide by asking the following and
   writing what you think, feel, or visualize. Is your Spirit Guide of a
   male or female dominant energy?

3. What era is your Spirit Guide from? (i.e. 1700s, roaring '20s,
   Atlantis, etc.)

4. What is the initial of your Spirit Guides name?

5. Ask your Spirit Guide to show you in your superconscious mind their full name (if you receive nothing, revisit this question over time, don't force it).

6. What lesson are you meant to be learning right now at this very moment with your Spirit Guide connection? (i.e. self-love, boundaries, stopping self-sacrifice, unconditional love, etc.)

7. Ask your Spirit Animal to reveal themselves to you. Yes, we all have a Spirit Animal. What animal do you feel, think, or visualize?

Further your connection here:

Ask your Spirit Guide for a specific sign. Remember there are no coincidences. Write your sign in the space below after stating the following, *"Now that we are connected, show me a sign in my physical world that you are listening and are present by _____. Thank you."*

Here are some examples...

Show me a sign in my physical reality by having someone walk up to me with a purple shirt; having an owl appear; showing me the word "love" on a billboard; have your name (Spirit Guide) pop up on the radio, in a movie, or on a commercial.

Catch the drift???

This is a great practice to help you get into the routine of flowing with your Spirit Guides and guidance. I would use this exercise over time to meet your other Spirit Guides. Now, the key is to trust it!

Use this space to write any additional thoughts about connecting with your Spirit Guides:

SPIRIT GUIDE MESSAGE

In a quiet place free from distractions, take six deep breaths and clear your mind. I want you to ask your Spirit Guide that you just met in the previous exercise to give you a message for the questions below. Let whatever comes to your mind, using my 3 to 5 Second Rule, flow directly onto the paper. Don't stop, don't break, and don't question it.

1. What is the meaning of your presence in my life right now? Why are you with me in Spirit?

2. With your guidance, what is the most important lesson I need to learn in my present life right now?

3. Please show me in my vision what it is I need to be doing to learn this lesson.

Note: *Spirit Guides come in and out of our lives over the course of our life experience. This means that assigned Spirit Guides will enter our lives at any given moment when Divine timing is right for us to learn a valuable lesson. When the lesson is complete, the particular Spirit Guide assigned for that lesson may move onto other responsibilities and another one may enter. Some Spirit Guides will remain for your entire human life experience. Hence why I stated earlier that growing and evolving your soul is a life-long process and experience. You will be a lifelong student of the Spirit world.*

CHAPTER SEVEN

TRUSTING YOUR INTUITION

There is a big misconception that as soon as we ask for a sign or when we are seeking guidance, that poof that the Divine will answer will automatically and quickly appear. We tend to be impatient as humans, so we think the Spirit world works just as fast and quick as in the human world. This couldn't be farther from the truth. Divine answers don't speedily get sent to us on our time. Not all answers are meant to be given fast and quick. In fact, I will go as far to say sometimes no answer is still an answer.

Signs may appear. Signs may seem to come and go. Signs may relate to whatever it is you are asking or thinking about. But that doesn't always mean you will have the full answers and guidance in that very moment. It is an energetic process we are dealing with when it comes to guidance and signs. I tell clients to be very clear in their inner knowing before taking action based on a sign. Better yet, don't overthink every sign you get either. Patience with the Spirit world is of the utmost importance to allow you to receive a bigger picture regarding your question or guidance you are seeking.

Once you get into the momentum of receiving your own guidance, one major rule I have taught for over a decade is:

MOTHERELLA'S 3 TO 5 SECOND RULE

*ANYTHING THAT POPS UP IN YOUR HEAD WITHIN
3 TO 5 SECONDS IS ACCURATE GUIDANCE.
DON'T OVERTHINK IT.
DON'T SECOND GUESS IT.*

~ Motherella

Follow this rule, practice this rule, make this rule part of your daily life, and you won't ever second guess yourself. Practice makes perfect.

People often ask me, "Well, how do I know what I am feeling is correct?" My answer is, "Your strongest feeling and your strongest energy are correct" When you know…you know. Stick with your intuition and you cannot be steered wrong.

True guidance and trusted intuition with guidance have no attachments to a response or outcome. If you reject an answer because you don't like the guidance, well that is too damn bad, lol. Take the guidance you get whether you like it or not, learn the lesson, find the purpose, and make the necessary changes or shift. Also, do not "will" your own guidance just to trick yourself into thinking it is correct. When Spirit keeps bringing you the same answers and the same signs over and over and over again, that is because you aren't listening.

When this happens, I say this, "Don't be a sitting duck for the Universe. Become the action and the must to make a change or shift." So, don't keep asking the same questions for your guidance until you get the answers you desire. This is failing your own intuition and more importantly you are failing your own self to have the life you desire.

I have encountered so many who people presumably believe that they are getting higher guidance when, in fact, it is the exact opposite. I have seen this first-hand in many people, clients, and students. I can read this negative energy from a mile away and the funny thing is that they aren't even aware they are doing it. They just think it is accurate. Low vibration guidance, which is guidance that is filled with warnings, negativity, worry, fear, etc. are NOT Spirit Guides nor superconscious guidance. It is your ego or that person who is offering their guidance through their ego. Also, anyone who needs constant recognition from you for the "guidance" they are receiving for you or feel they need to be "rewarded" because they were "right", isn't trustworthy guidance from a real psychic medium. Why? Because trustworthy guidance and psychic mediums channel and give messages from Spirit and leave it at that. Spirit is their validation, not a human. This is why you will want to learn to trust your own guidance that you receive from your Spirit Guides.

This also works in the reverse. If you are offering guidance through what you believe are you Spirit Guides and you are giving guidance with fear, worry, warnings, negativity, etc. you are working from ego rather than Spirit. I recommend further training and development because you are doing no service to others and more importantly failing your own abilities.

How do you separate ego vs. intuition to trust intuition and guidance? It is a good start by being humble and open to the possibility of being wrong. Harnessing this skill will shut down the ego over time and will allow you room for error and development. Yes, it is okay to be wrong! Working with intuition is a GPS, a guidance, not an absolute. Accuracy takes years to develop, so again, keep learning and practicing.

As I mentioned earlier, when you are trying to ask or receive guidance and if you don't get the answer right away, so be it. Move onto something else in the meantime and re-ask your question a little later in the day or week. Wait until you feel you have received a sign from your Universe before moving forward. Remember, it isn't on your time to receive an answer, only the Universe's time. Again, do not "will" your answer just because you want it. If you are pushing and forcing guidance, it doesn't mean you are getting it and if you do, it will not be correct. True guidance is a natural flow.

Asking for guidance is like planting a seed in a garden. Nourish and watch it grow over time. Yes, friends and family can have a good knack for guidance, but it won't ever be what you can trust and know from deep within. Don't ever lose sense of what is right for you because of others.

Trusting your intuition is difficult and very subjective for everyone. To trust your ego vs. intuition you must first understand what the definition of ego is. Now, I know there are many definitions formulated, but here is my definition of ego:

"Ego is part of your subconscious mind that has a nagging voice and never stops talking you into the opposite of your true desires. Ego is fear-based and filled with worry. Ego loves to live in low vibration and has a strong connection to our 3D world rather than the 5D dimension. In fact, your ego thrives and fuels itself through fear. Your ego stores everything from your past and pretty much imprints and embeds these subconscious negative thoughts and mythical beliefs, which have a vast effect on working with your higher self and true authentic version of you."

~ Motherella

Your ego does the following:

- Makes you feel ungrounded
- Makes you feel fear, worry and despair

- Sends you negative thoughts
- Sends you negative, fearful "warnings"
- Makes you feel there are consequences
- Messages come through harsh, mean, angry or yelling
- Makes you misinterpret signs
- Makes you disconnected from the Universe and the Afterlife
- Makes you feel 'hyped up"

Ego automatic writing does the following:

- Puts you in fear, worry and despair
- Gives you negative thoughts
- Sends you negative, fearful "warnings"
- Makes you feel there are consequences
- Messages come through harsh, mean, angry or yelling
- Makes you feel like you cannot achieve what you want
- Talks you out of seeking your heart's desire
- Inflates your ego rather than motivate your soul's desire
- Is judgmental
- Encourages fear and doubt
- Makes you worry
- Responds in an angry manner
- Criticizes you or others
- Reinforces limitations
- Separates you from your higher self

Your intuition does the following:

- Makes you feel calm and peaceful
- Allows signs to flow from your thoughts to the physical experience

- Makes you understand that when coincidences appear, it is because your thoughts or statements are connected to the Universe, Afterlife, signs, and messages
- Allows the signs to keep happening or repeating
- Makes you feel strongly connected to the Universe and the Afterlife
- Validates your thoughts and feelings
- Gives you a strong inner knowing
- Allows you to channel messages without questioning the answers
- Helps you to interpret your signs and synchronized events

Intuitive automatic writing does the following:

- Is uplifting and motivating
- Is calm and peaceful
- Flows freely from mind, to hand, to paper
- Is usually the first thing that pops in your head or within 3 to 5 seconds
- Feels loving
- Feels light
- Give a strong emotional bond
- Allows you to know you can achieve anything
- Give you the inner knowing that the world is limitless
- Is trusting and accepting
- Exudes love and forgiveness
- Is all-centered and infinite
- Feels peaceful
- Encourages oneness
- Is fueled with love

Let us reflect on Chapter Two with regards to the level of consciousness to help you gain trust of your intuition.

Now, let us look at how the superconscious differs from the subconscious.

SUPERCONSCIOUS GUIDANCE:

Superconscious guidance makes you feel calm and peaceful, not anxious or scared. So, ask yourself, do you feel excited or restless? True guidance brings a calming acceptance of the information. You also gain clarity with guidance.

If you are seeing or feeling different alternatives or even receive this guidance in dreams be sure you are knowing the difference between superconscious guidance and subconscious influences. When you are starting out, I always, ALWAYS say, "Don't interpret your dreams or get into depth with your dream in the beginning or you will end up going backwards with your development."

SUBCONSCIOUS GUIDANCE:

Subconscious guidance is unclear, muddy, and foggy. This means projection of your own ego. And, this should not be trusted. Your superconscious is very clear, bright, and colorful with clarity and radiance where your subconscious is suffocating, sabotaging, fear based, etc.

True guidance makes you feel joy from within yourself, not seeking joy from the outer self. True guidance makes you feel free. This must be practiced over time. Intuition is always growing and developing into a clear inner knowing, therefore, it takes years and years of practice to develop.

I recommend you avoid making big decisions if what you feel and/or think is inner guidance presents itself as cloudy or unclear. Re-read that again! Wait until you have full inner knowing and strong trust of your true guidance before making the decision.

The best approach to this development is to begin practicing with small decisions first and build your trust over time. Learn to harness that inner power of knowing your gut. If you are doing the right thing, you will feel strong and clear. If you are not, you will feel resistance and frustration. I call this, "blocked flow."

Three important rules when unveiling your intuition and learning to receive guidance are:

1. There are NO ABSOLUTES!
2. Just because you are guided to do something, doesn't make it right for everyone else to follow your same guidance.
3. If you aren't getting guidance when asked, don't blast your way through it or force it. Let it go and come back to it.

Because intuition is soft, quiet, and calm, many people ignore signs, disregard their gut instinct, and shut down guided thoughts and answers. **HINT: the quietest voice is the correct one.**

Because not all guidance flows purely simple and easy, sometimes you must take steps that feel uncomfortable. This is good, because in order to trust your own guidance you must first get comfortable with your inner knowing until it develops over time to a "for sure" feeling and inner knowing. This is how you trust it. Most people don't want to be wrong or fail, but you will never get developed, grow, or evolve if you are always trying to be right.

Another important rule to follow for yourself is that just because you are intuitive or are receiving guidance for yourself or others, it doesn't make it okay to project yourself onto other people. This is very important so listen up or re-read this sentence. If you are providing unsolicited advice or guidance as well as creating disharmony around you when you speak of "guidance", then you are not giving true guidance. Be respectful of your unveiling and understand the respect of flow with the Universe and Spirit guidance at hand.

The disharmony you or anyone can create by offering unsolicited guidance can also be because people have a disbelief and a misunderstanding of what intuitive or spiritual guidance is. These people may have a strong free-will and strong ego. If the guidance you are giving is not trusted, then in turn you aren't giving guidance at all, but rather projection of your beliefs. So again, if your guidance is creating a lot of disharmony, then you need to check yourself and check your ego. If you felt a "ping" of energy in your gut, mind, or felt chills, etc. as you were reading that last paragraph, I can assure Spirit is talking directly to you.

Finally, giving into society, fads, and risk-taking behaviors isn't guidance. This means you are going along with society's general consensus or behaviors within the human population. To help you through this, ask yourself this, "What have people of wisdom done?" That may be your best bet in deciding between true accurate guidance you can trust or doing something ego has driven you to do.

Most importantly, a note to remember: Guidance doesn't change with outward circumstances EVER, period, end of story. Guidance isn't dependent on external anything, only internal. True guidance from superconscious will make you feel so damn happy.

Intuition is always growing, evolving, and adapting to your current need. Therefore, get into practice and know that your intuition is an ongoing development throughout your human life. It never stops and will never end until your human life ends.

Also, very critical, so listen up…

If you keep rejecting your guidance, your opportunities, and your signs over and over because you want to constantly question the Universe to prove to you, show you, and validate you time and time again while you remain a sitting duck, your Spirit Guides will eventually stop responding. This is not because they are abandoning you; this is because you are ignoring the guidance, refusing your guidance, and rejecting it. So, they will step back, take a break, and allow you to decide between free-will of choice and free-will of guidance. Decide wisely!

TRUSTING YOUR INTUITION

The following exercise should be done quietly in your personal sacred space without any external noise or distractions.

Take six deep breaths, then read and answer the following questions with the first response that comes to you.

Do not question, "Is this right?" "Is this me or ego?" "Is this really true?"

Just write what comes to mind and let it flow resistance free!

1. When you ask yourself a question, do you get an answer in your mind or a thought or feeling right away? If yes, describe how. If no, why?

2. When you receive an answer for a question, do you second guess it? If yes, why? If no, why?

3. Do you get a "vibe" about people, followed by a reason why you have the vibe? If yes, write how. If no, why?

4. Do you second guess your decisions? If yes, why? If no, why?

5. Are you worried about making a mistake or failing? If yes, why? If no, why?

6. Do you seek guidance from outside influences and make your decisions based on their responses? If yes, why? If no, why?

7. When making a big decision, do you take time to ask yourself if this is right or do you impulsively decide? Write why.

8. Would you call yourself an intuitive? If yes, why? If no, why?

9. Do you wish to develop a stronger connection with your higher self and direct guidance? If yes, why? If no, why?

10. What three steps will you take right now to unveil your intuition deeper and strong and connect with your own guidance.

11. How many times have you received the same signs or guidance and ignored it? Write how you did.

SELF-EVALUATION

On a scale of 1 to 10 with 1 = the weakest and 10 = the strongest,

how would you rate trusting your intuition right now?

Rating: _____

CHAPTER EIGHT

EXPERIENCING SPIRIT

Children are more receptive to the Spirit world than adults. I find that as people get older, we go from being so open and clear with our intuition to being completely shut off and shut down. Children are born spiritually awake; over time they become spiritually asleep.

Children have better receptivity, strong intuition, and the ability to connect with Spirit is because of the laissez-faire superconscious as a child. They don't care if Spirit is real or not. They just know that Spirit exists. Fantasy vs. real isn't even in question. Children don't need validation.

Adult humans put themselves into a subconscious spiral and hype up their energy. This results in questions such as, "OMG, I felt something" or "OMG what is the Spirit trying to tell me?", or "OMG what does the sign mean?" This hyped up energy completely reverses the entire point of connection and then they lose the ability to simply and calmly connect with their higher self and Spirit. This type of energy needs to be tamed, harnessed, and controlled or you will never get true guidance and connection.

So, the difference is that a child intuitive is already intuitive and can instantly connect with the Spirit world. Adults must retrain their intuition and connection. As children grow older, they lose their access to their natural-born gifts of intuition, higher self, and psychic mediumship abilities. Adults must learn how to re-connect with the Spirit world.

If adults could resist their overzealous controlling minds and disempowering beliefs, imagine the guidance that would flow! They would have a deeper, more meaningful faith and connection to Spirit. Instead, humans demand proof, validity, and physical evidence. Huge, HUGE issue with our human world. We live robotically because of this.

Our Divine senses of hearing, feeling, seeing, smelling, and tasting all receive Spirit messages. Most of us have only ONE sense that we are attuned to: gut instinct, empathic, mediumship, feeling, intuitive mind (aka third eye) etc. My explanation of "third eye" is, *"the space between your brow in relation to your 6th Chakra that is your gatekeeper to your superconscious and Higher Power connection."*

WAYS OF CONNECTING:

FEELING: Emotional or physical connection with Spirit. This is how most people connect with Spirit.

How to tell your feeling Spirit? You will feel:

- Love, happy and warmth.
- Safe (even if you feel a sense of negativity, danger, or bad feeling).
- Disembodied smells or tastes, voices, and/or visions.
- Temperature changes.
- Someone touching your hair, back, neck, face, etc.
- High energy, then feeling tired right after.
- An inner knowing that "this is really them".
- Repetitious signs and serendipity.
- Sense of a particular departed loved one
- The connection experience which feels natural and is coming freely.

For purposes of this workbook, I will not indulge into a long chapter about bad "Spirits" but because many will be wondering about this as they read through this workbook, I feel that the signs of such Entity should be noted. At no point through this workbook will you connect with a low vibration energy. The only way to do so is by eliciting these Spirits through ghost hunting, Ouija boards, witchcraft, summoning or stirring up bad Spirits, or partaking in any uncontrolled connection with the dark, evil Spirit world. Paranormal and psychic experiences don't take over the human unless you are asking Spirit to use your body to do so. Again, don't fall into fear and the hype!

HOW TO RECOGNIZE LOW VIBRATION ENTITIES:

- Feel cold, chilled, and prickly
- Afraid and panicky
- Unfamiliar feeling
- Unpleasant smell like sulfur or death
- Sexual encounters or fondling
- Ice cold room
- Sense of feeling alone
- Forcing or willing the experience to happen

SPIRIT GUIDANCE THROUGH SUPERCONSCIOUS THOUGHTS ARE:

- Consistent and repetitive
- Reveal guidance or problem solving
- Positive and empowering
- Instructive and include action or steps to take now
- Ideas that energize you
- Random thoughts after prayer, manifesting, etc.

- Are logical and make sense

SPIRIT GUIDANCE THROUGH EGO THOUGHTS ARE:

- Discouraging or abusive
- Worst-case scenarios
- Depressing or frightening

As I have mentioned numerous times in the previous chapters, every human can connect and communicate with Spirit. Again, in my opinion, all humans are natural-born mediums and psychics. Not all humans share the same levels of gifted abilities either. Those willing to believe, trust, listen, develop, learn, and gain knowledge can put the kick back into any intuition that has been suppressed. Trying too hard to make a psychic mediumship experience happen for you will block your ability and reverse the process. Acting desperate, straining, or having self-doubt are also deterrents to your intuitive guidance and connection. Lastly, being anxious or fearful or even negative thinking, "I won't be able to" or "I can't do this" will also block you.

The more you relax and learn to quiet or calm the mind, the better you will connect. That is why it is important to practice meditation daily and write in your journal. Also, once you stop worrying about if your connection is real or not, watch how fast you learn ego vs. higher self. Don't discount your intuition. Trust yourself. They key is to listen to your gut instinct and pay attention to your red flags without ignoring them.

"ALL CHILDREN ARE BORN WITH AN IMMEDIATE CONNECTION TO SPIRIT. THE IGNORANCE OF THE UNDERSTANDING FOR THE SPIRIT WORLD, COUPLED WITH THE INABILITY TO GUIDE, TEACH, AND TRUST THE BELIEF OF THE SPIRIT WORLD SUPPRESSES THE CHILD'S INNATE ABILITIES."

~ MOTHERELLA

Take a moment to think about your childhood.
Did you have any Spirit experiences?
If yes, write about it briefly here.

EXPERIENCING SPIRIT EXERCISE

1. Sit in a quiet space away from all distractions and external noise.
2. Close your eyes.
3. Take six deep breaths and calm your mind.
4. Think of ONE family member that you would like to connect with.
5. Envision that family member in your psychic mind (third eye – between your brows) coming through a beautiful white diamond of bright light.
6. Feel their presence as if they are right in front of you or next to you.
7. Now, embrace them in your psychic mind and envision giving them a hug.
8. Wait a moment to feel their presence. Use your senses here to experience a smell, a thought, a message, or even a light touch. You may begin to feel chills or goosebumps, you may feel the room temperature changing, or you may begin to get emotional. It is okay to cry.
9. While the feeling of their presence is with you, do not become afraid or fearful because you will break the connection. Instead, remain calm and enjoy the moment. Your ego will want to tell you this isn't real or that it is scary. Trust me, it is real and should not be scary. This is a beautiful moment to experience.
10. When ready, tell your deceased loved one thank you for connecting.
11. In your psychic mind, begin to release them by envisioning them going back into a beautiful white diamond of bright light.
12. Take six deep breaths and when you are done open your eyes.
13. Write about your experience feeling Spirit on the next page.

My experience feeling Spirit...

CHAPTER NINE

SIGNS ON A DEEPER LEVEL

Outward signs are also guiding you. These are a great personal tool to flow with for guidance. Signs are strictly individualized. Signs you receive will not have the same meaning or connection for another person. Though there may be similarities in receiving them, signs are highly individualized and will not be the same for everyone. This makes the connection with the Spirit world complicated. However, as you unveil your intuition and practice your own intrinsic natural-born gifts of intuition, you will begin to develop your own Spirit language and Spirit dictionary with your higher self, Spirit world, and physical world.

Here is an example. Let's say you keep seeing the numbers 111 over and over again. That 111 can be a repeated "hello" from your Spirit Guides or Angels, letting you know they hear you, we are with you, helping you, and guiding you. Or, it can be an answer based on numerology to a burning question or desire because 111 (based on human writings and studies) is that you are spiritually awakening and beginning your journey of enlightenment.

This goes the same for Spirit Totems or Spirit Animals. Let us say you keep seeing hawks frequently. That hawk can be a symbol of your Spirit Guide or even a sign from your loved one. Hawks symbolize the ability to grow and develop your intuition and work through our third eye and expand our third eye vision. Therefore, once you unveil your intuition and work through your inner guidance you receive, you will know and be able to decipher between which is which.

Signs from the Universe and Afterlife are mysterious synchronized events that happen to us in our physical world.

WHAT IS A SIGN:

- A way of connecting us to the Spirit realm
- The Spirit world letting us know that the Universe and Afterlife are always around.
- Your Spirit guides, Angels and departed loved ones sending you the message that they hear you, see you, and love you.
- That you are on the right path

WHAT IS A SYNCHRONIZED EVENT:

- Meaningful coincidences
- The linking and connection of your intuitive mind with the physical reality
- The Universe and Afterlife sending signs repeatedly or in sync with your feelings or thoughts to let you know they hear you, see you and connect with you.
- That you are on the right path and to continue to move through the process
- To trust the process
- Validation of your thoughts, feeling and desires

Why do I need to know my signs when unveiling my intuition? Because signs will:

- Enhance your Spirit Guide, Angels and Afterlife connection.
- Help you to grow, evolve, and strengthen your natural-born intuitive, psychic, and mediumship abilities.
- Allow you to flow with the Universe and Spirit guidance for your highest good and live an authentic life.
- Give you non-verbal guidance to let you know you are on the right path.
- Provide you with higher wisdom and knowledge.
- Enhance your faith, trust, and co-existence with your own intuition and guidance.
- Provide validation of your thoughts being brought to fruition in your physical reality.

You do not have to be a professional intuitive, psychic medium, or healer to receive signs. All humans receive signs. There is this crazy notion out there that you must be a psychic or a medium to understand signs. NOT TRUE!

Every human is blessed with the gift of intuition. Therefore, every human can receive signs and understand the meaning of their signs. That is why I stated in the previous chapter, over time you will learn to develop your own language with Spirit.

"JUST BECAUSE YOU GET SIGNS DOESN'T MEAN THAT IS THE RIGHT DIRECTION. SIGNS CAN MEAN THE EXACT OPPOSITE. PATIENCE AND TIME WILL ALLOW IT ALL TO UNFOLD."

~ MOTHERELLA

Flowing with your signs is a good way to begin unveiling your intuition and working with your own language with Spirit. Your "sacred journal" is the place to record and write in your signs and synchronized events.

When receiving signs remember to:

- Let go of your mind control
- Let go of HOW or WHEN you are going to receive a sign
- Be aware and acknowledge unexpected coincidences
- Do not overthink the sign
- Do not allow EGO to interpret the sign

Motherella's Validation Names as a sign:

For decades I have received "validation names" from deceased loved ones during people's readings. In my readings, a validation name is the deceased loved one's way of showing proof that they spoke to us during the reading. That loved one or loved ones (if I am channeling more than one deceased loved one) will orchestrate, also known as synchronize, the validation name Spirit gave to manifest itself into the physical reality of the person I am reading for. I absolutely LOVE these types of signs. My track record based on the hundreds of thousands of readings and all of my testimonials has been this: the "validation name" I give in a reading always, ALWAYS, comes to manifest in the person I am reading for physical reality within 24 to 48 hours. Only a handful of times has it taken time past the 48 hours for the validation name to appear. What this boils down to is, as soon as the decease loved one gives me a validation name for you, you will meet someone with that name, hear that name, or see that name within a very short time and out of the blue. My clients LOVE this! I always tell whoever I am reading for that when this happens, stop a moment and say, "Thank you_____" (to whichever deceased loved one gave you that validation sign).

I also receive validation names from Spirit Guides. I receive this type of "validation name" when a person in the human world is connected to an event or situation that is about to take place in the future to whoever I am reading. For example: I will hear the name Jake as a connection to someone getting a new job. So, I say to the client, "Okay, when you hear the name Jake, either Jake will be the one to get you the job, interview you for the job, work at the job, or it may be the connection to the job itself somehow." Make sense? Shortly thereafter, wahlah, the name appears. The client is so surprised!

Motherella's 3-Digit Code as signs:

This is literally my favorite sign of ALL signs! Here is the deal with this. Since I began readings, I would be given three numbers by the decease loved one. These are random numbers given to me by Spirit in no particular order. I kid you not, those three numbers always add up and equal the decease loved one's birthday, death day, and birthday or the anniversary day of the person I am reading for. In fact, just recently, I started getting four digits from Spirit in no particular order that when added up together equals the same as stated, but includes an extended family member of the person I am reading for, such as a husband's or grandchild's birthday or anniversary.

My clients eat this up and love this because it is such a personalized sign from their deceased loved one. As soon as the code is given, they begin to see the code everywhere. (i.e. license plates, clocks, receipts, etc.) I have numerous testimonials about my 3-Digit Code. In fact, when I am doing live videos on social media or have a room full of people at one of my shows, you will see people asking me, "What is my 3-digit code from my Dad or Mom?"

I want to also explain this: everything in the Spirit world is broken down to single digits. This means that most of the time, Spirit wants use to add up, NOT SUBTRACT, two or more numbers to get a whole number. For example: 15 equals a 6 (5+1=6 not 5-1=4)

These following pictures are examples of how my 3-Digit and 4-Digit Codes are given to me by deceased loved ones in a person's reading.

The first picture is:

The deceased loved one was the father of the woman I was reading for. He gave me the number 414.

His daughter who I was reading for has a birthday of 4/22.

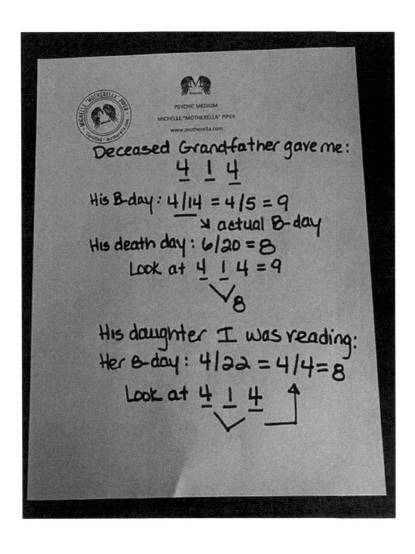

The second picture is:

The deceased loved one was the daughter of the man I was reading for. She gave me 125.

The Dad I was reading for has a birthday of 3/14

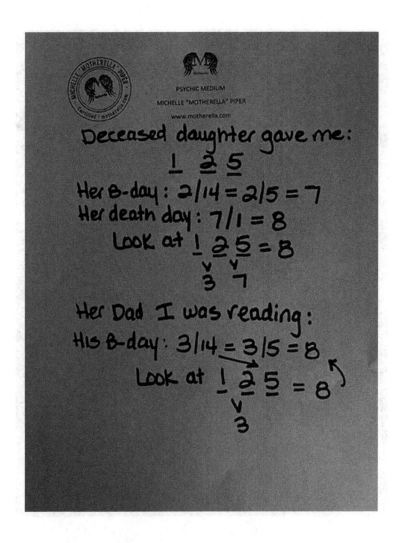

The third picture is:

The deceased loved one was the husband of the woman I was reading for. He gave me 7192.

The wife I was reading for has a birthday of 11/16 and they were married on 2/10.

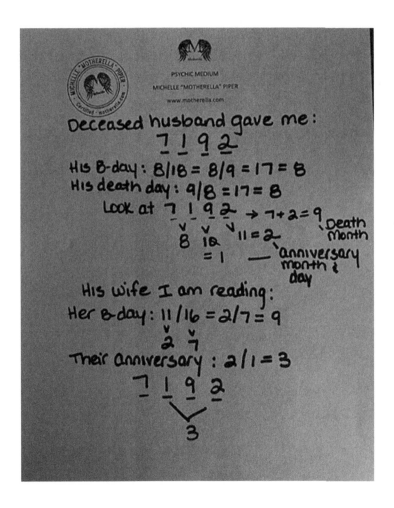

With so many signs being brought to us from the Spirit world, it is nearly impossible to understand and learn about them all. However, I do my best to help others to develop their own language with Spirit, their own Spirit dictionary, and to understand their own Spirit signs. In my course, "Knowing Your Signs," we take a deeper look into the art of connecting, receiving, understanding, and interpreting your signs. You can register for this course at motherella.com.

"THE MOST BEAUTIFUL EXPERIENCE IN OUR PHYSICAL WORK ARE THE SIGNS OF OUR DEPARTED LOVED ONES."
~ MOTHERELLA

SIGNS ON A DEEPER LEVEL

1. When you think about something, do you see signs about that thought on billboards, TV commercials, or through people bringing up conversation regarding that thought? Write about a time it occurred.

2. Do you frequently receive signs such as cardinals, hawks, pennies, or feathers randomly crossing your path? Write about a time it occurred.

3. Do you trust your signs and synchronicity events when you receive them? If yes, why? If no, why?

If you said yes to all three, welcome to unveiling your intuition and connection with your Spirit world!

EXERCISE TO CONNECT WITH YOUR DECEASED LOVED ONE

Take a moment of think about one to three decease
loved ones you may want to connect with (these
can be immediate family and friends).

Below place their name and month with date of birth (if
you can remember) in the space below. Leave the year out.
Spirit cannot bring you signs with that many numbers.

I am connecting with:

Name:

Date of Birth: _____ (month) _____ (day)

Name:

Date of Birth: _____ (month) _____ (day)

Name:

Date of Birth: _____ (month) _____ (day)

Now, state the following to connect with them:

"Good morning (or afternoon or evening) _____
(deceased loved one's name). I am excited and happy to connect with
you today. When I am thinking of you, feeling you, or wanting to talk
with you, please show me your birthday _____ (write
the birthday) on clocks, license plates, receipts, addresses or let me
hear your birthday in my physical world as a sign you are around. I
love you and thank you!"

Don't intentionally go looking for the birthday numbers because you
can manifest them in on your own. Let it flow in a natural energetic
state and be surprised! As you begin to witness these signs, record them
below.

Write the date you saw your deceased loves one's birthday.
I saw your birthday on _____.

**Write what you were thinking about or what you were doing while
you received the sign from your deceased loved one.**

Write the date you saw your deceased loves one's birthday.
I saw your birthday on _____.

Write what you were thinking about or what you were doing while you received the sign from your deceased loved one.

Write the date you saw your deceased loves one's birthday.
I saw your birthday on _____.

Write what you were thinking about or what you were doing while you received the sign from your deceased loved one.

CHAPTER TEN

FOLLOWING YOUR INTUITION

Superconscious is part of your higher self and your own intelligent force. Your intuition and guidance won't do you any good to just receive it. You must act on it. Acting on your superconscious creates the flow of energy that opens you up to multiple doorways of opportunities, shifts, and changes. Like I said over and over, "Don't be a sitting duck."

As you continue to practice the "act" of flowing with your intuition, you will use your intuition all the time without even having to ask or think about it. Most people are afraid to act because they want proof, validity, confirmation, or results first. That is a robotic way of living. This level of hesitancy will eventually block your flow and dry up your guidance. The more you use guidance and trust it, the more it will flow and open you up to love, happiness, joy, health, wealth, and abundance.

Don't wait to act. ACT!

You are not always in control of guidance. Your superconscious guidance comes in ways that is out of your control. When you ask for it, even unintentionally, it will begin to flow.

Don't be discouraged by obstacles and blocks. Obstacles and blocks are our navigation and GPS to get it right. None of our guidance is a straight shot. There are curves, ebbs, flow, mountains, hills, speed bumps, and roadblocks to pivot us, move us, and shift us until we get it right.

Flow can also be affected through a "Spirit psych". Lol. Yes, that is exactly what it means. The Spirit world tests us, so they sometimes "psych us out" to see if we are paying attention and listening. You may have a strong feeling or vision for something that is leading you in that way, then wham a block occurs. This is your internal cue to you ask yourself, "Is this something I really desire?" "Am I really supposed to be doing this?" Again, your guidance and answers are for your highest good, not what you think is for your highest good. Your Spirit world knows best.

Obstacles can be challenges to your own willpower testing your free-will. Hence, no blocks, only opportunities to put more energy into accomplishing your goals, dreams, and desires. Obstacles can balance your inner power and give you courage to act on your guidance with flow while allowing yourself to be redirected or corrected when needed. Trust me, this is a way of life and a way you will surely enjoy living by.

Never presume your direction is 100% as your guidance is not a one-time occurrence. Your guidance can change as you flow. Remain humble and don't be so presumptuous. When you aren't clear or don't feel it 110%, don't go full force with it. Try it out first. Test the waters. Have patience. Remove resistance. Silence the mind. Wait it out. The inner knowing will come with full speed ahead. Your green light will shine. Trust me, you will know.

Even though actions can be done with goodwill and intent, your "common sense" can get in the way. Your common sense may have told you to do move in one direction, when in fact, it was the wrong direction. That is because a "realistic" approach based on society's norms, limited thinking, and mythic beliefs about yourself, your path, and your purpose is not accurate guidance.

So, follow this:

Without strong feeling of clarity = don't go full out in that direction.

Wait until you feel a strong inner knowing of YES before acting. The mind is capable of many games. Exercise good judgement always. The Universe is governed by laws that need to be observed. If your mind says, "jump of a cliff", your common sense and "law of gravity" need to be observed.

When it comes to flow, again, your flow isn't always what others should flow with. When making decisions simultaneously with partners, spouses, co-workers, teammates, etc. don't persuade people just because you have the guidance to do something. Your guidance is not for everyone. Instead, ASK THEM FIRST! Does this make sense to you? Does this feel right to you? Should we try this? If you want people to join in what you are doing, ask in a way that leads them to their own understanding. NO force. This creates great harmony between humans and indirectly will help others practice their own intuitive guidance.

Have a healthy respect for the possibility of error with regards to others. Guidance shouldn't be offered unless asked. Share guidance as an alternative, not an absolute, unless asked.

This applies to you too. If you feel you are going in the wrong direction, stop, pause, take a moment, and ask for the guidance again. Trust me, you will be redirected if necessary. To live in true guidance and attunement of our guidance, we must live in a way that flows, trusts, has courage, determination, and balance. This is the art of flowing with your intuition.

"LISTEN QUIETLY. WITHIN YOURSELF IS TRUE GUIDANCE."

~ MOTHERELLA

PRACTICE FLOWING WITH YOUR SPIRIT GUIDANCE

Ask your Spirit Guides the following questions and write the answers IMMEDIATELY to the first thing that pops in your head.

Remember my 3 to 5 Second Rule for this exercise.

Note: This should not be answered from thought, so don't sit and think about these questions. If you get NOTHING as a response, that is okay!

This test can be done repeatedly at various times. So, if you get NOTHING as a response, either keep moving past the question to another question or take a break and come back to the exercise at a later time.

1. Am I on my path and purpose?

2. What can I do to align with my path and purpose?

3. What is the most important personal fears, false beliefs, and mythical thinking I need to work on and/or remove from my subconscious mindset?

4. What do I need to learn to value myself?

5. What do I need to focus on right now to trust myself and Spirit?

6. Am I making the right choices in my career? or Do I need to find at career that brings me joy? If you are currently not working, when will I find a career?

7. When will I travel to _____ (insert your favorite destination you have on your bucket list)?

8. Am I in a loving, solid, trustworthy, faithful, and aligned life partnership? If you are single, ask what do I need to learn about being a life partner?

9. When will I be financially stable or debt free?

10. What do I need to do to align with money flow and financial freedom?

CHAPTER ELEVEN

FALSE GUIDANCE

Your ego distorts your intuition and communicates false guidance to you. Most humans live primarily in ego guidance instead of through their superconscious guidance. You cannot expand out of your limited reality and live the life you are meant to live if you remain in limited consciousness controlled by ego. Your ego is very misleading. To better understand the ego driven way of false guidance, let me explain the four parts of consciousness:

1. **The mind** – observes and sees reflection; reflects through senses to conscious
2. **The intellect** – divides and defines knowledge for understanding
3. **The analytical** - separates the world around us and loses sight of unity or all as one.
4. **The ego** – steps in and divides even further the separation between mine vs. what's not mine

The final step, the ego, is the cause and creator of your distorted reality (3D). Your hold back. Your self-sabotage. To make the consciousness even more complicated to work through, the four parts combine into a process in which you can have emotional reactions to. This confuses you, complicates things, and further deflects and distorts your reality.

Your emotional response can make you react too quickly, and that puts you into a mental, emotional, physical, and spiritual spiral that can cause your mind to gear into overdrive. As a result, your overthinking is amplified. Your emotional reaction to ego creates a rippling effect. This is when the real delusional mind process begins which misleads you from your true inner guidance to false guidance.

Make a mental note that intuitive Spirit guidance does NOT equate to personal feelings. False guidance occurs when you are too personally involved. So, when it comes to filtering out what is real vs. what is ego, heed the advice to remove all personal feelings, don't react, and allow the guidance to flow without your control. How? Again, meditating and journal writing until you are so quick and fast to receive your intuitive guidance through your superconscious.

This understanding is particularly important when it comes to manifesting your dreams and desires. Having a false reality, false perception, and false guidance will block you from manifesting.

For those who are unclear about manifesting, my definition of manifesting is: *"Expanding your superconscious mind through feeling and expression, both visible and invisible, that works simultaneously with the Universe to boomerang your intentions of those dreams and desires to you."*

Your dreams and desires do not interfere with your ability to see, think clearly and be objective; your ego does. When you project dreams and desires from the heart, that is not intuition because you want things to come out in a certain way. When you expand your superconscious and allow yourself to feel your dreams and desires, you are energetically sending out intentions that you know these dreams and desires are your birthright in your physical reality. The Universe begins responding to this expansion and begins throwing signs your way that you are on the right path and that your answered prayers are on their way. Granted, you must take the steps and do the work on your part. Practicing manifesting can also assist with your ability to separate true guidance from false guidance.

Numerous people follow false guidance by staying in unhealthy relationships. I cannot tell you how many clients I have worked with who insist on thinking that the Universe and their Spirit Guides are bring them signs to stay in an unhealthy, toxic, and loveless relationship. Here is an example: A client is in a toxic, unsupported, unhealthy, co-dependent, passive/aggressive, addictive relationship. The client is beyond miserable and unhappy. Yet, they stay, using every excuse imaginable (i.e. money, career, fear, children, no place to go, etc.) Then, they ask the Universe to show them a sign if they should stay. Within days, they begin to receive signs on billboards, at the mall, on t-shirts, etc. that show "you are loved" or "love is all around". Now, they tell themselves that the Universe's sign to them is letting them know that they are loved and should stay in the dysfunctional relationship. ABSOLUTELY FALSE!

Let me attest for the Spirit world that no way, no how, would your Divine guidance, Angels, Spirit Guides, or whomever else you pray to allow you to remain in a toxic, unhealthy, sacrificial, disallowing relationship. The sign that client received simply meant that they are loved by their Divine, Angels, Spirit Guides, and departed loved ones and that is that. The answers already reside within that client; the true divine guidance is already within them or they wouldn't be asking to stay or leave to begin with.

Another false guidance asking is, "Show me the right choice." Then, they are shown the correct choice, but continue to remain in the same exact position with cement feet holding them down. Then they ask again for a sign, only to receive the same answer. Yet, they still stay planted and emotionally paralyzed. Then, they ask again with the same response over and over again. This will only lead to false guidance because of their own free will. That free will is free will of choice to not listen to their guidance and ignore their signs.

Ignored signs are your ego at work. Your ego loves to keep you planted in fear. Fear fuels your ego. This means, false guidance. Because deciphering between accurate and false guidance takes time and experience, I have taught my 3 to 5 Second Rule to help harness this skill while developing your intuition. If you missed it in the previous chapter, here it is again:

MOTHERELLA'S 3 TO 5 SECOND RULE

This is for you to practice daily.

*"ANYTHING THAT POPS UP IN YOUR HEAD WITHIN
3 TO 5 SECONDS IS ACCURATE GUIDANCE.*

DON'T OVERTHINK IT.

DON'T SECOND GUESS IT."

~ Motherella

Anything past the three to five seconds is you willing an answer or trying to convince yourself of it. This is exactly the point when ego steps in.

Remember, your subconscious mind and ego are not true guidance. Please don't allow yourself to be influenced by false guidance. Practice removing your mythical thinking and false beliefs through meditating and journal writing. If you don't, your idea of your reality will be false and misleading which will never help you live a life of joy, happiness, wealth, health, and abundance.

False visions are a major obstacle to your superconscious true guidance. I see this with a lot of people who "think" they are a well-trained intuitive and psychic medium. Visions that are not from the superconscious, but rather the subconscious, are merely hallucinations. These people like to tell themselves or trick themselves into believing they are talking to Spirit Guides, Angels, and departed loved ones when in fact they are communicating with their own ego. Your mind, body and soul must be energized, or in a high vibration, to receive true guidance. You will not receive true guidance when you live in a low vibration.

False guidance in a low vibration comes from:

- Negative thinking
- Negative energy
- Connecting through ego
- Being high or taking mind altering prescription drugs
- Feeling fogged or being unfocused
- Pretending or hallucinating
- Failing to do the inner work
- Lacking in meditation or other healing modalities for self
- Lack of sleep
- Poor Diet

You also cannot tap into superconscious if you cannot relax and control your body. I see this a lot with people trying to meditate. There should be no fidgeting when connecting. People who claim to hear, see or feel Spirit guidance and do so with a negative attitude are in fact arrogant, self-centered, and misrepresenting the Spirit world.

Another way to receive false guidance is when you give too much meaning and energy into outward signs. Those signs become superstitions rather than guidance. There is no need for the hype. Trivial signs are not Spirit signs. For example: Hitting your funny bone, tripping on a rug before walking into a home or store, stubbing your toe, or losing your car keys. What this CAN mean is that as a human, you need to slow your roll because you are moving too quickly in life. Inexplicable things do happen in the human world that do not always have a meaning, sign, or an attached lesson as the outcome. This is called the human world. So again, don't become so robotic that you begin to live your life as if everything is a sign. You will drive yourself crazy. See signs as a Spirit game and don't take signs so seriously.

"LET YOUR GUIDANCE AND YOUR SIGNS REFLECT YOUR STRONG IN INNER KNOWING BEFORE YOU ACT ON IT."

~ MOTHERELLA

In addition, if you are an avid believer in psychic mediums, you should never depend on psychics for your every move. Psychic mediums, that is TRUE psychic mediums, are meant to be Spirit advocates of your own guidance. They should be helping you find ways to connection and help you achieve your own guidance through that connection. A psychic medium can help guide you with your past life lessons that need to be learned, as well as, manifest and carry out your heart's desires. You should never become dependent on them. Even though psychic mediums can be viewed as a human Spirit Guide, there are no absolutes with their channeled guidance. Why? Because YOU are the creator, the shifter, the mover, and the game changer to your own life. Humans create their own blocks, their own sabotages, their own issues. False guidance vs. real guidance is on you.

This is a perfect time to help you identify the difference between true vs. false psychic mediums. If a psychic is real, they should be able to tell you something that pertains to your life without you having to speak in detail. The following statement made by you is a prime example of such truth and accuracy if a psychic medium is giving true guidance that is real, "There is no way you would know that!" BINGO! No, it was not a coincidence.

If any psychic medium claims you have a spell on you or that you are cursed, I am telling you do not pay them a dime! If you are with a fake psychic medium, he/she will tell you that your life is doom and gloom. He/she will also try to persuade you into thinking that if you give them hundreds or thousands of dollars, they can break a curse, create a spell, rid the spell, or even make someone love you. Now, let me be clear, I am not knocking those who believe in voodoo work, hoodoo work, witchcraft, etc. If that is what you are seeking out for guidance, then so be it. I am solely speaking on behalf of a true vs. fake psychic medium.

A fake or phony psychic medium will NOT provide you with clear, accurate guidance bathed in light and love. Instead, they will put the fear of the Divine in you and make you feel awful or even scared. Most likely they are giving you deceitful information. Not good! My advice to help you identify a non-authentic psychic medium is that a true authentic psychic medium will not seek you out for services by saying, "You NEED a reading ASAP" or "Spirit told me to tell you that you need a reading". Beware of this, especially on your social media. If you see a message that says, "DM (direct message) me right away" or "I have a message for you, contact me", umm NO! Do not allow fake and phony psychic mediums to prey upon you. A true, authentic psychic medium knows and trusts that the Divine, Angels, Spirit Guides and loved ones will bring people to them energetically who truly need their services.

A real psychic medium WILL NOT:

- Ask you multiple questions
- Be vague or hold back information
- Give you their opinion
- Instill fear of death or dying
- Tell you you're cursed or have a spell
- Sound scattered or change the reading based on your response (because the information should be coming directly from source)
- Leave you in worry and fear (which is not the same as "forewarned is to be forearmed")
- Seek you out
- Prey upon you

A real psychic medium WILL:

- Give you solid information from your loved ones and Spirit Guides (that information will either pertain to your life, or someone surrounding your life)
- Give you signs to look for from your loved ones
- Give you the feeling that you are immediately connected with your loved ones, Spirit Guides or Angels
- Make you feel loved and guided
- Help you with your path and purpose
- Provide you with guidance to make change, identify signs and give tools to work on your own spiritual and intuitive evolvement
- Trust that the Universe will bring them the people who need a reading or Spirit connection through you
- Won't tell you what you want to hear, but rather, what you need to hear

So, when unveiling your intuition, I recommend using a psychic medium as a navigation or guide for you through their readings, teachings, or courses to help you further your intuitive gifts. As I said before, psychic mediums are human Spirit Guides because they are channeling your Angels, Spirit Guides, and departed loved ones. They are the interpreters of Spirit.

"A TRUE AUTHENTIC PSYCHIC MEDIUM WOULD
NEVER MAKE YOU DEPENDENT ON THEM. INSTEAD,
THE PSYCHIC MEDIUM WOULD HELP GUIDE YOU
TO BE DEPENDENT ON YOUR OWN SELF."
~ MOTHERELLA

FALSE GUIDANCE AND LOW VIBRATION CHECK LIST

This exercise is the most amazing self-evaluation for your Spirit connection. This exercise will let you truly evaluate where you are in your conscious level and evaluate where you are between low vibration, subconscious mind (ego and 3D) vs. being in a high vibration, superconscious mindset (higher self and 5D) connection.

Answer "yes" or "no" to the following questions:

1. I always say, "I'll believe it when I see it." _____
2. I see situations that happen to me as glass half empty. _____
3. I am constantly full of fear and worry. _____
4. I am always fearful or worried for others, especially my family. _____
5. When good things happen to me, I feel guilty or that I am undeserving. _____
6. I often say, "This is too good to be true!" _____
7. I feel "life" is happening to me rather than for me. _____
8. I struggle with trusting the "process" of my life. _____
9. I try to control the outcomes in my life and/or I am always trying to "fix" things. _____
10. I feel I am always in an emotional, mental, physical, and spiritual prison due to my stress and chronic worry and fear. _____

EVALUATION RESULTS

If you answered yes to any questions, then you are in the subconscious 3D mindset.

If you are split between all 10 questions, then you are stuck between the 3D and 5D consciousness and are in the 4D consciousness.

If you answered no, or answered all questions on the right side, then you are in the superconscious 5D mindset.

Fast ways to move from a low vibration to a high vibration. I have many ways; this is just a few QUICKIES:

1. Meditation.
2. Exercise.
3. Journal writing.
4. Smudging or saging your personal space. Using smudge sticks to sage your home to clear stagnant, old, stale, and negative energy. You don't need any "ritual" to do a personal home smudge for a quick vibrational shift because smudging works on its own.
5. Breath work: Take quick small deep breaths by inhaling and exhaling. When done, repeat this affirmation: *I refuse this low vibration I am feeling right now. I only allow positive energy to flow within me and around me. As of now, I am balanced. My vibration is high!*

CHAPTER TWELVE

THE DOORWAY TO YOUR SUPERCONSCIOUS

The more you seek to follow intuition and get your own guidance, the more you will flow. The stronger your energy remains in a higher vibration; the better positive energy will flow into your life. To make this energy shift in your life, you must allow yourself to access your superconscious and get out of subconscious thinking. Adjusting your thinking to access your superconscious is basically mentioned in all the chapters throughout this workbook. Take each of the chapters and read them thoroughly. When you are done reading the workbook and doing the prompts, do it again. Treat this workbook as tool for your gateway and doorway to your superconscious thinking. Know that you must study and practice to begin living this way of life.

All life is in unity with the superconscious. The more you live in the vibration of unity with your superconscious mind, the less analytical you will be. Find a relationship between things in this human world and don't see anything as separate. Don't dwell on the length of differences either; that is human thinking. Remember that your rational mind is your disunity. The rational mind can assist with solutions in life, but your intuitive mind is where your clear answers are.

Once you begin to really turn up or level up your intuition and Spirit guidance, don't use your inner guidance as a claim for arguing your point to others. Why do I say this? Because rest assured once you begin to access the doorway to your superconscious and your intuition begins to level up, you will also be leveling up your vibe and guidance for others around you. These people may not be open to you and your newfound Spirit world. Lol. They will also need to start somewhere, so maybe gifting or recommending this workbook would be a good place to start before pummeling them with your (quote-unquote) "guidance." Instead, help them to begin their process with your suggestions.

If you happen to be using this workbook with a friend or family member, please be aware that not everyone unveils and develops their intuition at the same pace. In fact, accessing the doorway to your superconscious may be slower or faster than another person depending on your level of intuitive practice. Hence, intuition is highly individualized (even though every human is gifted with it upon birth). Also, putting the time and inner work in will be different for you than it is for others.

The doorway to your superconscious has very easy access. The only block is yourself, not the Universe or Spirit world. The access to your superconscious is always available to you. Your access is a thought or feeling away.

Steps to the doorway of your superconscious:

1. Ask from superconscious level.
2. Wait for heart-centered response by using Motherella's 3 to 5 Second Rule.
3. If you receive no guidance, pose another question or wait a bit and come back to it.
4. Guidance comes after setting your mind, body, and soul into motion. Make a move and don't be a sitting duck.
5. Continue to realign and readjust yourself as your guidance begins to flow. Re-ask your questions as needed.
6. Be open to making shifts and changes.

7. Remember there are no absolutes.
8. Release and let go. Don't control it. Let it all flow.
9. Trust the process and the timing.
10. Keep working with your higher self and your natural-born gifts of intuition over the course of your life.

Meditation for continued development of your intuition will:

1. Retrain your mind to step into your superconscious daily.
2. Get you into the skill of listening to guidance before doing.
3. Keep your mind open and receptive.
4. Help you learn to sink into the vibration of meditation without thinking your way into meditation.
5. Retrain you to feel true guidance and inspiration because you cannot think your way into true guidance and inspiration.
6. Increase your ability to receive wisdom and guidance through meditation by easier access to your superconscious.
7. Help you acknowledge your inner truths with a calm mind and open awareness.
8. Help you receive and perceive answers without you creating them.
9. Help you listen to your higher self while taming your ego.
10. Help you achieve the skill of stillness while receiving inspired thought.

Deeper states of meditation peel away the layers of your past that reside in the superconscious. Meditation releases tension and attachments that block you from healing. Meditation helps you practice mind control. The more you want to access your higher self, spiritual guidance and connection with the Spirit world, the more you will make meditation and journal writing your way of life.

Meditation for intuition is a:

1. regular practice and lifestyle.
2. mind, body, and soul exercise.
3. sacred practice in a personal sacred space.
4. way to frequently balance your Charkas.
5. tool for breath work.
6. way to control you mind while keeping your body still.
7. way to focus and concentrate without fidgeting or dealing with external noise.
8. way to bring you peace, joy, serenity, and happiness.
9. way to create inner wealth that can mirror your outer wealth.
10. way to create all dreams and desires.

As a side note, anytime I teach meditation, I let students know to keep a journal next to them. It is a great habit to get into. When you access the superconscious, the sky is the limit. Being in the routine of writing down everything you feel, see, and hear in your meditation will be mind-blowing and powerful. You will amaze yourself when looking back at your journal entries! Your Spirit Guides and Angels are always in continuous communication with you and, trust me, they have a lot to say. Meditation is a great way to keep you in constant flow with them.

MEDITATION TO ENHANCE YOUR SUPERCONSCIOUS CONNECTION

In this exercise you will reserve time to
practice this mindset meditation.

I recommend meditating a minimum of three times a week if you
are going to truly do the inner work provided in this workbook.

This meditation is strictly for mind control.

1. Sit or stand in a comfortable place without any external distractions or noise.

2. Use a stopwatch, timer, alarm or clock and set it for three minutes.

3. Close your eyes and relax your body.

4. Breathe slowly in and out while "feeling" your breath entering your nose and chest. Exhale slowly as well. This is going to energetically calm your body down.

5. Envision a white diamond bright light in your psychic mind (third eye – between your brows).

6. Now, do NOTHING but hold that vision in your psychic mind as long as you can or until the timer sounds.

7. Practice stillness with no sound, no noise, and no thoughts.

8. If you break concentration, go back to envisioning in #5 and #6. If the timer goes off, while holding this vision – then congratulations! You are able to calm the mind.

9. When the timer goes off, take six breaths, break concentration and open your eyes.

10. Continue to work on this exercise as much as possible. Each day and each week increase your time until you can reach five minutes in pure silence and stillness.

This is a BIG challenge, but much needed to deepen your connection with your higher self and Spirit guidance through your superconscious level of the mind.

CHAPTER THIRTEEN

DIVINE ANGELS 101

Angels have been portrayed in various ways throughout our world depending on which religion or culture. The term, Angels, is interchanged with other Beings in the Spirit world. To begin to understand the hierarchy of Angels, we must describe each of the Angels that surround us. The hierarchy is like that of an employee in a company, where the Angels are an employee of the Divine. The Divine is the boss. I think these descriptions will help you understand the differences between these supernatural Beings.

ARCHANGELS (GUARDIAN ANGELS):

The Archangels oversee all other Angels. For me, Archangels are much stronger and more powerful when I am communicating with them. Personally, Archangel Michael and Archangel Raphael are who I call upon quite frequently. Everyone is capable and able to receive help from Archangels despite their religious beliefs. They just need to be directly addressed and asked to help.

You never have to worry about calling upon your Archangels because they can energetically transmute between time and space. Archangels can be in multiple places at various times. Yes, they can help limitless requests. Your Archangels are a thought or feeling away. No formal prayer or ritual is needed. We all have connection to our Archangels.

Not all people have the same Archangels, however; they vary from person to person.

Remember, the Archangels are energy Beings and move rapid-fast like the speed of light. To get a better understanding, I want you to view Archangels as the energies outside of a large fishbowl; that fishbowl is the planet Earth. Inside that fishbowl are schools of different fish species. Those fish species are comprised of humans. Archangels are gigantic energies compared to our human energies which are tiny specs.

ASCENDED MASTERS:

Ascended Masters are supernatural Beings who walked the Earth as leaders, teachers and healers who have completed their incarnations. Ascended Masters have the highest wisdom and have mastered becoming immortal. They have attained their ascension and will help other human lightworkers to do the same.

NATURE ANGELS:

Fairies are known as mythical and suspicious; they are very misunderstood. They are our environmental helpers. Nature Angels help humans on Earth maintain our land, our bodies of water, our eco system, our wildlife, and our atmosphere.

GODS AND GODDESSES (MYTHOLOGY):

Gods and Goddesses are referred to as immortal, supernatural Beings with sacred gifts and powers reigning over the human world. Many people who follow mythology worship these supernatural Beings.

SPIRIT GUIDES:

Spirit Guides help us with our path and purpose. They support and guide us through our human life experience. They are our direct guidance and communication when needing answers to our direction in life. Spirit Guides cannot intervene when free will of choice is exercised in place of our true guidance.

SPIRIT TOTEM/SPIRIT ANIMALS:

Spirit Animals and Spirit Totems are also our Spirit Guides. These Spirit Animals protect and guide us on our journey through this human life experience. Examples include the following: wolf, eagles, hawks, dolphins, panthers, etc. A Spirit Totem is also a Spirit Being that comes into our human life experiences depending on the direction we are heading, to help us complete our tasks in this lifetime.

DECEASED LOVED ONES:

Deceased loved ones cannot assist us with our path and purpose; instead they help with our emotional, physical, and mental well-being. Our loved ones are always around us loving us and protecting us.

They assist and help our healing process. Though our deceased loved ones provide support, they are bound by Spiritual Laws, therefore, their ability to help us and/or intervene is limited.

Note: Spirit Guides, Archangels, Spirit Animals can come in and out of our lives based on where we are in our path or when certain lessons have been completed. That is why unveiling your intuition and connecting with your Spirit Guides must be practiced and is a lifelong process.

You can live your best life for your highest good and you will keep ascending!

There are many books, blogs, articles, and social media posts about Spirit beings in the Afterlife, such as Ascended Masters, Archangels, Guardian Angels, and Spirit Guides. All Spirit beings in the Spirit realm serve a purpose in our human life, and that is to protect and guide us. In theory, Angels are known as messengers, protectors, and guardians for us in our human lives. Though the term Angels is interchangeable for some people, Angels play different roles in our human experience as they are helpers and direct messengers from the Divine (i.e. God, Source, Creator, etc.)

Some organized religions instill fear into people who want to connect with these other Spirit Beings. That fear blocks the connection to these Divine Beings and limits people from attaining their true authentic self and limitless life. It is also taught through some religions that calling upon the Divine and Divine Angels can be bothersome. You should never be fearful nor feel that you are bothering your Angels from Above. Your Divine Angels are there to help you. That is their duty as Spirit Beings. Divine Angels help you navigate, and they are part of your internal GPS. The only limit to their help is your own lack of faith and trust.

Divine Angels will help you grow and evolve, then shove you out of your own way when it comes to fear, worry, sadness, despair, and any other negative perpetuating thought or feeling. But it is up to you to listen and follow. Divine Angels help keep you on track. They help you fulfill your purpose and learn your personal lessons. They can intervene upon your asking or your request, however, you need to give them permission to do so. Honor the Spirit Law of Divine intervention. You must ask for the Divine intervention for them to intervene.

Here is an example of how I ask for Divine intervention (you may use as a template for you or make your own):

"My Archangels and Spirit Guides, I am asking for Divine intervention with regards to_____. I release and surrender this to each of you. I let go of all control. I ask that you blend, heal, or shift the energy for what serves my highest good. Thank you and I love you."

We are all blessed upon birth with the two choices for our path. That path is either free-will of choice or free-will of guidance. We are all capable and able to choose which direction we want to go in while living our life experience. We can choose a path of free-will where we choose to ignore our higher conscious connection, soul path, and spiritual connection or we connect and flow with it. This is something I have been teaching for a long, long time! I have drawn my theory on numerous client readings.

My theory is this:

Free-will of choice = path = consequences, setback, blocks, negativity, worry, fear, etc. (3D reality)

Free-will of guidance = path = love, health, wealth, abundance, connection, etc. (5D reality)

Spirit Guides are assigned to us from birth and stay with us until our last breath in our human life. Some Spirit Guides have never lived as "humans" on Earth. Remember, Spirit Guides are energetic or light

Beings that are assigned to us at birth from the Divine from different dimensions of your Universe. Spirit Guides who have lived long ago as humans on Earth have gone through major transformation, ascension, and training as their incarnation process has become complete to become a Spirit Guide. This is very similar to the process of the Ascended Masters.

We all have Spirit Guides and Guardian Angels. Your Spirit Guides are not the same Spirit Guides for other people. The number of Spirit Guides and Angels are infinite. Also, we all have Guardian Angels, but those Guardian Angels are different for each human.

If people are unaware of their Spirit Guides and Guardian Angles that is only because they aren't connecting with them. To connect, unveiling your intuition, accessing your higher self, and opening your superconscious are the keys to opening your connection with them.

Guardian Angels are often interchanged with and referred to as Spirit Guides. However, in the many decades I have been channeling the Afterlife and performing readings for hundreds of thousands of people, I have always seen, felt and heard Divine Angels as distinctly different.

Spirit Guides and Guardian Angels nudge us to make the right choices, follow our path and purpose, learn lessons, and keep to our highest good. It is a wonderful blessing to be able to connect and communicate with them!

TEST YOURSELF

Let's test your memory of terms below. Circle True or False:

1. Fairies are myths and not part of your Nature Angels.
   True | False
2. Gods and Goddesses are immortal, supernatural Beings with sacred gifts and powers.
   True | False
3. Spirit Guides give the same guidance as loved ones.
   True | False
4. A Spirit Totem or Spirit Animal can be my Spirit Guide.
   True | False
5. A deceased loved one can help us on our path and purpose.
   True | False
6. Ascended Masters are supernatural Beings who have walked the Earth as leaders, teachers and healers and have completed their incarnations.
   True | False
7. Archangels are energy Beings and move rapid-fast like the speed of light.
   True | False
8. Spirit Guides oversee the Archangels.
   True | False
9. Spirit Guides only help with our emotional, mental, and physical well-being.
   True | False
10. Our deceased loved ones are bound by Spiritual Laws.
    True | False
11. Spirit Guides, Archangels, and Spirit Animals can come in and out of our lives based on where we are on our path or when certain lessons need to be learned.
    True | False
12. Ascended Masters have the highest wisdom and have mastered becoming immortal.
    True | False

ANSWER KEY IS ON THE NEXT PAGE.

ANSWER KEY:

1. F

2. T

3. F

4. T

5. F

6. T

7. T

8. F

9. F

10. T

11. T

12. T

Now that you understand these terms, let's talk more about connecting with your intuition through connection.

CHAPTER FOURTEEN

UNDERSTANDING DIVINE ANGELS
AND DEPARTED LOVED ONES

Departed loved ones in the Afterlife are often thought to be our Guardian Angels. Though this is partially true, refer to the descriptions (Chapter Thirteen) to know the difference between Guardian Angels, (aka Archangels) and how our departed loved ones protect us. Archangels as our Guardian Angels play a much higher and important role in our human life experience than other Angels or Spirit Guides.

Guardian Angels, Spirit Guides, and departed loved ones can comfort us when we are in a low vibration (i.e. sad, lonely, tired, frustrated, disappointed). They are also there in our happiest, most joyful times sharing our feelings of joy, laughter, love, health, and success. We are most connected to all these Divine Angels when we live in a high vibrational energetic state of happiness and love.

Angels and Guardian Angels do not have a human gender. Their energies can seem to feel or appear as a reflection of male or female energy. That is why many drawings and writings portray Archangel Michael, known as the Angel of Protection, holding a sword.

Divine Angels and all Spirit Beings in the Spirit world have personalities and characteristics. When trying to connect with your Spirit Guides, stay gender neutral and allow them to put forth their male or female energies. Also, everyone has at least ONE Spirit Guide, but the majority of us have multiple Spirit Guides. What this means is, you might have seven Spirit Guides, but have only connected with five of them. Your sibling may have 10 Spirit Guides and may have connected with only one of them. Your Spirit Guides are meant to connect with you on your own. No psychic medium should tell you who your Spirit Guides are! That defeats the whole purpose of your connection. Psychic mediums are only allowed to guide you to them. This includes your Spirit Animals.

When it comes to connecting with departed loved ones, this will and can take time; that is because you do not need to know who your departed loved ones were in your physical human experience to have departed loved ones, (aka ancestors) connect with you. Your departed loved ones have various duties and assignments in the Afterlife to help protect and guide you and your family generations.

Upon death, our soul leaves the human body and begins its journey back to its origination to the Higher Power. Parts of our departed loved one's soul can re-incarnate. You may sense this with new babies born into your family where you feel they mirror a deceased parent, a grandparent, or a sibling.

When our departed loved ones arrive to the Afterlife, there is no human emotion or feeling that is carried with them. Our departed loved ones do not journey to the Afterlife with grudges, pain, anger, suffering, disappointment, etc. The departed loved one's illness, injuries, disabilities etc. from the human life totally disappear. There is no money and material items in the Afterlife. This is often why a psychic medium or medium wouldn't always pick up exactly on each loved one. Once they transition over, they are free from the human experience. When connecting and channeling, our departed loved ones will provide concrete clues that they are present other than how they passed (i.e. cancer, car accident, burn victim, murdered, etc.)

I often get asked in readings, "Are my loved ones okay or are they at peace?" The answer is, yes. Your loved ones are in an energetic space of a higher light frequency not a place. Therefore, they are always ok and at peace because there are no feelings in the Afterlife

Now, some might argue that there are evil Spirits, trapped Spirits, or Earthbound Spirits, which is true, but that is an entirely different discussion and does not fit into the content of this workbook.

Our loved ones do not want us to hold on to emotions and feelings of sadness, despair, grief, anger, etc. from their departure. Your departed loved ones can sense your mind, feelings, and connection through your heart. Though they are always around us to help us with our grief and healing, their end goal is to make sure we heal. It makes it very difficult for our departed loved ones to fulfill their duties for the Divine and Spirit world when they so desperately desire us to heal and try so much to help us.

Energetically, the only problem the Afterlife Entities have with humans are that we are oblivious to them or aren't listening. Lol. We as humans have a hard time following our path and purpose. Many people live with chronic anger or resentment. Humans struggle with forgiving each other. We live in a world of greed. Many live enduring pain and suffering. Lastly, many humans refuse to honor and take care of their physical bodies. Can you see why the Divine Angels have a much harder job than us here?! That is a lot of negative energy for them to deal with.

The soul is the only thing that leaves this earthly plane intact and in perfect health. Let me be clear, this does not mean that ending your life, taking your own life, or asking to go before your time will provide the same "energetic process" back to origination, because it doesn't. Though controversial and won't be discussed at length in this workbook, energies (souls) that force themselves to leave before their human life experience is complete may have some "unfinished business" to attend to and many more lessons to learn." So, their journey back to their origination to the Higher Power may be lengthened or they will quickly reincarnate again.

In my second book that I co-authored, <u>Hurt to Healing</u>, we referenced that the best way to clear the air with your departed loved ones is to write them a letter. You can communicate with them anytime or anywhere. That is why this workbook stresses the importance of meditation and journal writing. Both tools are very therapeutic and healing.

DECEASED PETS:

Your deceased pets are also guiding you and are always around you. Yep, your deceased pets are a thought or feeling away. The connection with your pets is a bond that will never sever, and you will remain connected for the rest of your human life. Many deceased pets in my readings come through like human souls. They have male and female energies, personalities, characteristics, behaviors, and appearances similar to our departed loved ones. Their characteristics can be maintained after death.

I have had many clients talk about paranormal occurrences surrounding their pet's death. I have also had many clients talk about their current living pets feeling like they were human. That is because pets also have souls. Deceased pets can also be our Guardian Angels just like our Spirit Guides and Guardian Angels. Our pets love to infuse us with the Divine energy of love and companionship from the Afterlife.

LOSS OF A CHILD:

The loss of a child is one of the most devasting things anyone could experience. Most parents are overwhelmed with sadness and despair. Some parents feel guilty and are left wondering if they could've done something differently. Many parents feel that loss of a child was somehow their fault. Departed children go through the same journey as our adult departed loved ones. They too are free from any trauma, tragedy, illness, or difficulty here on Earth. (refer to Deceased Loved Ones in the previous chapter)

When connecting with a departed child, they love to bring pictures to life to let us know they are okay. In readings they often show me rainbows, items they played with, places they went to, or special stuffed animals to let the family know they are present and around. Most stillbirths, abortions, and miscarriages stay closely to their mother, father, and sibling(s) and can reincarnate to that next child. Sometimes these baby souls become human Spirit Guides as they reincarnate to another child being born into the family.

"THERE ARE DIFFERENT LEVELS OF GIFTED INTUITION AND PSYCHIC MEDIUM ABILITIES, BUT THAT DOES NOT MEAN ONE CANNOT INTUITIVELY CONNECT WITH THE UNIVERSE OR THE AFTERLIFE. EVERYONE CAN. YOUR UNIQUE GIFT OF INTUITION ALREADY EXISTS WITHIN YOU."

~ MOTHERELLA

TEST YOURSELF

Let's test your memory of the terms below. Circle True or False:

1. Angels and Guardian Angels do not have a human gender.
   True | False
2. Divine Angels and all Spirit Beings in the Spirit world have personalities and characteristics.
   True | False
3. We only have ONE Spirit Guide.
   True | False
4. Only your departed loved ones you knew in your physical human experience will come through and connect with you.
   True | False
5. Upon death, our soul leaves the human body and begins its journey back to its origination to the Higher Power.
   True | False
6. When our departed loved ones arrive to the Afterlife, there are so many human emotions and feelings that are carried with them.
   True | False
7. There is no money or material items in the Afterlife.
   True | False
8. The connection with your pets is a bond that will never sever, and you will remain connected for the rest of your human life.
   True | False
9. Deceased children are free from any trauma, tragedy, illness, or difficulty here on earth.
   True | False
10. Souls that force themselves to leave before their human life experience is complete may have some "unfinished business" to attend to and many more lessons to learn.
    True | False

ANSWER KEY IS ON THE NEXT PAGE.

ANSWER KEY:

1. T

2. T

3. F

4. F

5. T

6. F

7. T

8. T

9. T

10. T

11. T

Now that you understand these terms, let's talk more about connecting with them.

CHAPTER FIFTEEN

PSYCHICS & MEDIUMS

Psychics and mediums are two different types of intuitive gifts. Many spiritual and metaphysical teachers and writers claim that every human is a psychic, but not all psychics are mediums. I disagree with this claim. In the several decades of my teaching and working with students from all over the world, I have taught people to access, awaken, develop and strengthen their psychic mediumship skills by learning to blend both at the same time. With that said, I have come to the realization and conclusion that all souls have the inherent gifts of both; we just need the proper guidance and training to access, blend, and develop our skills. I will, however, state this; not all people are natural-born psychic mediums at the same level.

Many people believe that mediumship is a spiritual practice. That is untrue. The ability to connect with Spirit lies within all of us and it doesn't matter if you practice it spiritually or not. Many times, our conformed thinking and organized religions sabotage us from being able to access and use these inherent gifts. Do some people have a stronger and deeper connection with the Spirit world than others? Yes! But that does not mean you can't advance yourself with a little help and training. I will also add that there are various strengths in the levels of psychic mediumship skills that use our senses. Not everyone has the same connection through their senses right away, but one can definitely grow and develop these abilities using their senses. These senses are known as "The Psychic Clairs".

Before we get into discussing the psychic clairs, let us understand the difference between a psychic and a medium.

PSYCHIC:

A psychic is a person who foresees the future, read minds, and can connect with Spirit Guides to help one gain clarity, wisdom, and direction into their path and purpose. Ex: when you will sell your home or when will you get a new job.

MEDIUM:

A medium is a person who can connect with the Afterlife, paranormal, and supernatural and provides connection with the unforeseen. Ex: they can communicate and bring messages from your deceased loved ones.

Both psychics and mediums use extrasensory perception to communicate with Spirit. These abilities are known as the "The Psychic Clairs" and are defined below:

CLAIRVOYANCE:

Clear seeing and perception of the future. Also interchanges with the "sixth sense."

CLAIRAUDIENCE:

Clear hearing – being able to hear beyond the human normal hearing of a supernatural or Spiritual Being.

CLAIRCOGNIZANCE:

Clear knowing – this is a psychic's visual talent in which they can see timing frames, events, people, places, etc. beyond the human physical eye including past, present, and future. This clear knowing is interchanged with Divine knowing.

CLAIREMPATHY:

Clear **emotional** feeling and can feel other people's emotion and physical pain. A strong, hypersensitive psychic intuition that can feel energy of other people and Spirit. When channeling, a clairempath can bring forth a Spirit message as if they were still alive here on Earth (even though the soul leaves all feeling in the human world upon death.)

CLAIRSENTIENCE:

Clear **physical** feeling – ability to feel when touching an object, or when someone walks into a room, or a strong innate feeling or sense of something beyond the physical. "Inner knowing". This is often interchanged and blended with clairempathy.

CLAIRALIENCE:

Clear smelling of fragrance, odors such as sulfur, metal, food, flowers, smoke, spices, etc.

CLAIRGUSTANCE:

Clear tasting without substance in the mouth such as sulfur, metal, spices, blood, etc.

CLAIRTANGENCY/PSYCHOMETRY:

Clear touching and can extract information from inanimate objects such as deceased loved one's jewelry, artifacts, clothing, etc.

Psychic mediumship abilities that are suppressed and shut down can take years to develop. Having the proper training, practice, and development exercises can help you achieve accuracy and clarity. Practicing your gifts daily will build your confidence with your inner knowing and will help you receive your own channeled guidance.

The ability to blend both psychic and mediumship abilities together is the only way I teach people to develop an amazing connection to Spirit. Though, as stated earlier, there are various levels to these gifts depending on the individual's strengths and weaknesses, overall you will have a basic connection.

With that said, I must point out that not all psychic mediums perform readings the same way, nor will they communicate the same way. Every soul has their own individual connection with the Spirit world including their own Spirit language and Spirit dictionary. Though there are many courses and classes to help people tap into their strengths of these abilities, one must realize that not everyone develops, grows, and connects in the same way.

In my courses, I teach my students to create their own Spirit language and Spirit dictionary throughout their development. What this means is that they are required to journal how Spirit communicates with them. This is an advanced skill, but extremely important for interpretation of Spirit messages.

Here is an example:

When I am channeling Spirit, they show me movie reels in my head to explain timelines, dates, locations, and events. So, when I want to know timing such as Springtime, they may show me on an intuitive calendar the month of March or a number 3 which represents Springtime. While another student may see Easter eggs, grass, and sunshine to express Springtime.

This is why it is important to journal as much as possible during your unveiling, development, etc. because over time you will see a consistent pattern begin to flow.

Psychic mediums are the messengers, conduits, peacemakers, and guides for all humans in this lifetime. A psychic medium must have their ego in check to provide clear and accurate guidance without the need to be right. Guessing, bias, judgement, opinion, and making up ego stories is not channeled guidance, nor is it communication with Spirit. Again, this takes years of practice. The best way to gain reliability is through your personal testimonials from people. If psychic mediums truly want to help people in this human world, then they will commit to being honest in their skill set to stand out from the fake and phony psychic mediums in this world.

There is a difference with connecting with Spirit on a personal level vs. connecting that is done on a professional level. No one should practice mediumship to the public without formal training. It does no good and is not a service to others practicing as an untrained psychic medium. Even worse, an undisciplined medium claiming to help others can actually cause harm.

With that said, my disclaimer is that when you use this workbook and instantly begin to grow and develop, it does not mean you are ready to begin a psychic mediumship spiritual practice. Do not fail yourself, others, and most importantly the Spirit world by doing so unless you are completely ready, clear, confident, and accurate with this path and purpose.

When using this workbook, don't try too hard to make a psychic mediumship experience happen. Let it flow naturally. If you force it, you will block and reverse the process and can even shut down your intuition. Desperation, self-doubt, anxiety, and fear will also block this process. Everyone has the ability, so don't place unnecessary thoughts in your head such as, "I can't do this" or "This isn't true". Also, remove the negative thoughts about, "Is this connection real?" That is ego creeping in the disbelief. All connection is real. As you mature, grow, evolve, and harness these abilities, trust me, you will not question yourself again. Don't discount your intuition. Trust yourself. The more you relax, quiet, and calm the mind, the better you will connect. Again, practicing meditation is your best teacher for expanding your consciousness and harnessing your gifts.

Other tools you may hear about or see psychic mediums using during their readings to deepen their connection with Spirit may include:

- Angel, Oracle, Universe cards
- Pendulums
- Bay/tea leaves
- Crystals balls
- Crystals
- Coffee grounds
- Spells/energy work

There are other "psychic powers" that one can possess. These are some of the few I refer to when teaching students:

ASTRAL PROJECTION:

This is when you can project your consciousness outside your physical body and is often performed during meditation.

INVOLUNTARY PROJECTIONS:

Also known as out of body experience and a near-death experience. These terms are also interchangeable with Astral Projection. This often occurs via flight or fight response, fear, fright, feeling threatened, injury, harm, and some other traumatic experiences. Most of the time, an out of body experience is when someone has a near-death experience.

LEVITATION:

Lifting or rising into the air without support.

PSYCHIC SURGERY:

Often performed by energy healers as a way of energetic healing (aka Reiki or Energy Work).

PREMONITIONS:

Seeing or knowing future events prior to them happening.

TELEPATHY:

Communication between the psychic and another human's thoughts and emotions. This is also performed with animals.

AURAS:

A psychic power that can see a human or Spirit energy colors. A human's aura can radiate like a bubble or cylinder and can be quite expansive around that person. These are colorful vibrations that can provide insight into a person's emotional, mental, physical and spiritual energy. When I am communicating with Spirit, I have developed my own Spirit language and Spirit dictionary; I call this "My Spirit Auras". For me, Spirit shows me four aura colors when I am channeling, I see Spirit auras as: dark, grey, white and iridescent. This helps me connect with their dimensional journey and how they are transitioning back to the Higher Power. This is an advanced skill that will not be discussed in this workbook, but I felt the need to mention it because seeing Auras is not just for humans, but for the Spirit world as well.

Psychic mediumship is not intended to be a game nor a form of entertainment. Just look on TV and see how we have taken something sacred and turned it into a show. As I mentioned earlier, there are a lot of fraudulent psychics out there. Often, people associate psychic gifts with magicians which is completely ridiculous. We live in a world of facts and proof with just about everything in life. My advice is this, don't try to prove to yourself or to others that your abilities are real. Just trust it!

As a medium, we must remember that Spirit messages go through various wavelengths to get their messages across to us. Those messages can be slow or fast, distant or close, near and far, or low and high. That is why mediumship work takes years of practice and development for you to become accurate in delivering messages to others.

Spirits that want to "show" themselves through their energetic representation (i.e. male vs. female; young vs. old) will do so how Spirit sees fit, not the other way around. So many people who want readings from a medium have a high expectation that they will hear from who they want to hear from or who they knew and were associated with in their human experience. That is not how the Spirit world works. Spirits that want to come through will come through whether you knew them in this lifetime or not. Your ancestors are still part of your energetic connection.

In my readings, I can read an entire room full of 50 people where everyone gets read. Why? Because I don't play the fishing game that psychic mediums do for entertainment. My shows are this: write your two questions down and let's get down to business. Tell me who you want to speak with in the Afterlife and we will. I can assure you I will channel a message that is directed entirely for you and in which I have no way of knowing. Spirit always has the floor. They are in control. So, when someone asks me, "Does anyone have a message for me?" I often, chuckle and reply, "All Spirits have a message for you, including Spirit Guides, Angels, and your loved ones." Being specific at "calling in" of a departed family member, cuts through the chase so I don't have to fish through all the Spirits. A true authentic psychic medium doesn't need to validate themselves in a room full of people; that is Spirit's job.

Most people looking for a mediumship reading know who they want to talk to, or who they feel, or who they are getting signs from or who they are connecting with. These people want validation. They aren't willing to accept their intuition as valid, so they need confirmation. But that doesn't mean your job is to validate them. Your job is to validate Spirit.

It takes a lot of practice, training, trials and errors to attain confidence in this type of work. I teach my students to gain confidence and their own Spirit dictionary first before performing readings. That way no client nor someone wanting a message can steer you off your Divine messages. The messages will be directly from Spirit. Again, I cannot express this enough, a true authentic medium does not and will never need validation from any human for their channeling experience. The only validation they need is from Spirit themselves.

Also, you must remember that people will not receive a message of what they want to hear, but rather what they need to hear. Even when a message doesn't make sense to them at that moment in time, it will eventually. Trust me on this! Sometimes messages can come across vague and need further investigation between the psychic medium and Spirit. Again, this takes time to learn and understand. However, over these vague messages will make sense.

If Spirit's energy is too loud, too often or too much, it is okay to ask Spirit to slow it down. Spirit is in control of what messages they want to give, but you are in control of how to receive it!

For me, here are some of the ways I hear Spirit:

- Higher Power is very strong, loud, direct, and to the point.
- Archangels, Angels, and Spirit Guides are loud, direct, and to the point as well, but they do so in a more formal way as if I were in a room with teachers. They have an approach to "getting on track", making a shift, ridding doubt, fear and procrastination.
- Loved ones talk as if they are still here and alive

A quick note to decipher between you and ego:

- Your higher self sounds like our own voice.
- You will feel like you are condemning yourself.

Ego is a pain in the ass, abusive, fear-based, annoying, discouraging, paranoid, worried, overthinking, negative and depressing.

Things NOT to worry about when connecting as a psychic medium:

- Losing control like Spirit is going to take over your body or make your life crazy
- Seeing something fearful or that spooks you
- Being fooled
- Being punished
- Evil or wrong
- Being ridiculed
- Taking on too much energy
- Not being able to do it

THOUGHT THE ESSENCE OF PSYCHIC MEDIUMSHIP CAN BE TAUGHT, THE SKILL IS INTUITED BY THE INDIVIDUAL LEARNING TO DO SO.

~ MOTHERELLA

In the next couple of pages, I will be testing both your psychic and mediumship abilities and challenging you during the exercises.

A few things I want to point out:

1. You don't need to meditate prior to connecting
2. Connecting does not have to be a big production with crystals, candles, prayer, etc.
3. If this is new for you and you are just starting out, you will want to get into the habit of taking a minimum of six deep breaths until you become so advanced you won't have to. This process will help you relax and calm the mind to stop the mind noise and energetic chaos that can block your connection.
4. Reminder: everyone is able to connect with their natural-born gifts through thought and feeling.

TEST YOUR PSYCHIC ABILITIES

1. Have you ever felt something happening prior to it happening (déjà vu)?

2. When people ask your opinion, do you quickly see images and the answer playing out in your mind (head)?

3. Are you able to describe a place or even a room you have never been to before?

4. Have you had a thought of someone and soon after you ran into them, they called or messaged you?

5. You have an inner knowing (i.e. vibe) when someone is lying, being deceitful, or does not have good intentions?

PSYCHIC EXERCISE: CONNECTING WITH PRESENT AND FUTURE

These are fun exercises that will really test your
ability to expand your psychic abilities.

Remember, don't force the information just let it flow.

Remember my 3 to 5 Second Rule, whatever pops in your
head within that time is correct so write it down ASAP!

1. Pick a sporting event for this exercise (i.e. Football game, Basketball game, Soccer game, etc.) try to predict the score by writing the date of the game and predicted score below:

Date:

Home team score:

Opposing team score:

What was the final score?

2. Ask of friend or relative you can trust to work with you on this exercise. Have your friend or relative ask you THREE things about something they want to know that is coming up in their life (ex: if they are selling their house, will they get a new job, when will they find love, etc.).

Your friend or relative should be asking you in this format: who, what, where, when, why, and how.

Name: _____ Date: _____

Write their questions below:

Write your psychic responses:

In about a month, or over time – check your accuracy with this friend or family. Maybe even have they text or call you when the event comes to fruition to check your predictions.

Let's do some fun predictions:

1. Who will win the next presidential election? (this is a tough one because ego, bias, opinions will have to stay out of the prediction).

    Who will win?   _____

    Date of your prediction: _____

2. Try to pick the "Pick Three" or "Pick Four" lottery numbers for the next game. Don't make this a regular thing, this is just for a one time fun and is similar to the raffles they do for, "How many jellybeans are in the jar?". (Play responsibly if you play the lotto, if you have any addictive behaviors related to gambling, skip this exercise – this is only for fun). Good luck!

    Date of picking my numbers: _____

    My Pick Three numbers: _____

    Actual result: _____

    My Pick Four numbers: _____

    Actual result: _____

3. Take a deck of card. Shuffle them. Now lay them on the table and close your eyes. Try to visualize the top card you are about to pull and see if it matches your vision. You can continue to do this for each card until the deck is complete. This tool really helps to remove ego and focus on your psychic visualization.

    How many did you get correct?   _____

4. Take a high-profile case on television or news article, such as a kidnapping, murder, or someone looking for a suspect. Try to observe the case without knowing details just the basics. (The victims name and what happened). Then I want you to try and connect with the event, situation, location, victim, etc. Write down everything you feel, think, see, or hear in your mind. This exercise is to not be used to influence families, media, authorities, etc. The exercise is meant solely to help develop and grow your psychic vision.

My vision of this is:

TEST YOUR MEDIUMSHIP ABILITIES

1. As a child, did you have paranormal or supernatural experiences?

2. Can you feel a "presence" around you when thinking about a loved one?

3. Have you had unexplained experiences with electronics, lights, things missing, etc. after the loss of a loved one?

4. Have you had unexplained smells and aromas (such as your grandfather's cologne, or your mother's perfume, or flowers in the kitchen, or cigar/cigarette smoke in an empty passage seat, etc.) throughout your day, night, or while driving in a vehicle?

5. When you think of a decease loved one, does a song come on the radio, or do you hear that loved one's name that day?

6. When asking a deceased loved one for love, guidance, or help, do you feel you hear their voice in your mind?

7. Can you see unexplained movement or shadows out of the corner of your eye?

MEDIUMSHIP EXERCISE: CONNECTING WITH A LOVED ONE

Remember, this skill will NOT connect you with
anything negative. That is a mythical belief.

This exercise is to get you connect immediately with a past loved one.

I am challenging you here, so take you time
and do not force the connection.

In this exercise you will choose **ONE** decease loved one to
connect with (not a Spirit Guide). You may use this exercise
once for every loved one you want to connect with.

Do not try to connect with more than one decease loved one at a
time or you will have blended energies and inaccurate connection.

1. Sit or lie down in a quiet space with no noise and no distractions.
2. Close your eyes.

3. Take six deep breaths in and out to clear your energy and calm
   your mind.

4. Think about one of your decease loved one's.

5. Try to feel them with you or next to you.

6. Say hello to them by name. For example:
   a. A parent: "Good morning Dad" or "Hello Mom"
   b. A child, friend, sibling, or other relative: "Hi, Mary" or
      "Good evening, Joe"
   c. An animal: "Hi, Pumpkin" or "Hi, Snow"

7. Here is the KEY to connecting, just relax right at this point and allow the energy to come through. You may feel emotional, begin to tear up, cry, or feel an enormous sense of love, peace, and serenity.

8. Have a conversation. Don't let ego begin to work here by thinking this is you talking, or your own thoughts, or this isn't real, or you will deter the beautiful experience. Just simply talk. Ask questions. Tell them anything you want to tell them. Ask them anything you want.

9. Take your time and don't rush this experience.

10. When ready, tell them you love them, that you look forward to your next conversation, say "Thank you for coming through to me today".

11. End the experience by taking another six deep breaths before opening your eyes to clear your energy.

12. Before getting up, write down everything you just experienced on the pages provided.

MY MEDIUMSHIP EXPERIENCE

Name:_____ Date:_____

Write your full experience below don't leave out any details.
Write everything you felt, saw, heard in your mind, etc.

MY MEDIUMSHIP EXPERIENCE CONTINUED:

CHAPTER SIXTEEN

SCATTERED ENERGY

When learning to unveil your intuition or working through the psychic mediumship exercises, you may feel somewhat scattered or a feeling of "heightened" energy (like floating in the clouds). These are normal feelings and I assure you they are nothing to worry about. If this pertains to you, there are things you can do to keep you grounded (sort of pulling you back down to Earth, lol).

Here are my recommendations based on what I do or use:

- Hold, wear or place grounding crystals around you such as hematite, smokey quartz, and jasper
- Hold, wear or place protection crystals around you such as tourmaline, black onyx, and obsidian
- Begin a regimen self-care routine
- Practice journal writing
- Meditate
- Practice yoga
- Live a healthy lifestyle with exercise and a more natural, organic diet
- Consume a good amount of water daily
- Listen to your body when it says to sleep, rest, or take a break

Also, I often use a professional Reiki Master to clear my energy, attune my conscious expansion, and balance my Chakras. People need to stop thinking they can always clear themselves just by reading a book or by doing meditation from YouTube. Sometimes, you just can't clear your energy on your own, so consult the professionals to help you. A professional energy healer can help you.

You may be wondering why I mentioned the word, "attunement"? Just as you would tune a guitar, piano, or a car, for it to work properly while in use to deliver the best results; that goes the same for us. Getting rid of old, stagnant, toxic, muddled energy is needed frequently for the new to flow and for us to live in a high vibration keeping us in the 5D level of consciousness.

CHAPTER SEVENTEEN

BLENDING IT ALL TOGETHER

In my, "Unleash Your Psychic Mediumship" course, the most important final part of that course is to teach my students to blend all that they have learned into a strong and solid communication with Spirit. This is not an advanced skill by any means. What this means is, taking all of the information that you have compiled through the lessons and prompts to create your own language with Spirit and your own Spirit dictionary by allowing Spirit to show you how each of the following signs are represented in your psychic mind:

- Symbols
- Seasons
- Numbers
- Colors
- Plants
- Animals
- Personality traits
- Physical images & appearance
- Songs
- Phrases
- Word associations

We all can have the "basic" psychic mediumship skills, like many others. However, when using your psychic senses, it is individualized. You can learn from other mentors and spiritual teachers, but no two people have the same abilities, the same natural-born gifts, or the same way to connect. Remember, Spirit is in control.

Even with me providing many details in this workbook and giving you enough foundation and tools to develop, your learning journey will continue to become your own. You will keep evolving and growing alongside Spirit. The Spirit world will become your first and foremost teachers, mentors, and guidance from this point on. Yes, you can still read books, take courses, attend seminars, etc. But again, that is to just learn and consider the basics of what others have done in order to make it your own way.

As the blending with Spirit continues to happen day to day, journal writing will be extremely important and will need to become your best friend if you want to take your development seriously. Spirit will decide when they will come through, how they want to appear, and what messages or guidance they want to provide you with. So, learning the mechanisms, personalities, and details of your Spirit Guides will be necessary from here on.

Your Spirit Guide will show you:

1. Timeframes that are representative to you and them.
    a. Spring: rain for April, the #4 for April, Easter eggs or bunny, etc.
    b. Winter: snow, holiday lights, Christmas tree, the #12 for December, etc.

2. References of the Spirit world that will only make sense to you.
    a. Timing: can be in months, dates, years, or numbers
    b. Family members: a grandfather's cigar shown to you, a piece of jewelry shown, a vacation destination, etc.
    c. Music songs in your head: to represent an important message in the lyrics, the title, or a sign it will be played soon, etc.

3. Spirit will decide how they want to appear to you.
    a. They may "show themselves" in your third eye or mind.
    b. As an apparition or silhouette
    c. As an aura color
    d. Male vs. female energy
    e. Young vs. old

When you journal, write and record, you will see your dictionary and language with Spirit begin to develop. You will be able to track your progress with it. You can see your accuracy and clarity develop.

As you continue your practice, you will begin to see "movie reels" in your psychic mind (third eye – between your brows). You will hear messages in your head throughout the day. Yes, this is your connection and communication with Spirit, you are not crazy! Those who are very advanced psychic mediums, such as me, can see and hear Spirit externally. This advanced technique is not something you can develop or learn. This is an innate gift offered by the Divine and Spirit world.

As you continue to practice these skills over and over, eventually you will be able to hear and see Spirit in your Divine mind (third eye – between your brows) at every moment of the day. This is when you will need to harness your gifts through meditation and grounding by using some of the practices we discussed in the previous chapter. If it gets too much for you or you feel tired, take a break and go do something else.

I teach my students another advanced skill called, Motherella's Remote Viewing, which I have used in my professional career to locate missing items, helping with psychic investigations, and connect in detailed ways for families and people who have lost their loved ones to murder, kidnapping, suicide, adoption, etc. Again, this is an advanced skill that takes years of practice to develop. I wanted to make mention of it to show the possibility of growth and expansion of your psychic abilities over time.

For the purposes of this workbook, I want you to continue practicing the blending of all you have learned to meld with Sprit. Don't be afraid to push yourself and go further into your Spirit connection. If something doesn't make sense, ask Spirit to show it to you. Connect with Spirit on a deeper level to become accurate and clear on the messages you are receiving.

BLENDING WITH SPIRIT EXERCISE

Blending with a deceased loved one:

1. Choose a deceased loved one to connect with (i.e. a parent, child, grandparent.)
2. Call upon your deceased loved one by name: "Hello _____, I am so happy to connect today. I want to talk with you today about…."
3. Think and feel that loved one energetically with you and around you (refer back to Chapter Seven on how to know Spirit is around).
4. Once connected, ask your first question such as, "What was your favorite place to travel with me?" Spirit may respond by telling your or showing you a lake home, a country you both frequented, a honeymoon, a family trip, etc.
5. Go deeper with your loved one and further your connection by asking, "What was your favorite part of this travel with me?" Spirit may respond by showing you family game night, a firepit night singing songs, skiing, etc."

Catch my drift? BLEND and go deeper with Spirit!

Blending with your Spirit Guides isn't limited. Don't feel you can only ask one question for your path and purpose; ask multiple questions. If you have not "met" one of your Spirit Guides yet, that is perfectly okay. This exercise still works with results because your Spirit Guides are always around and always connecting with you whether you have formally "met" them or not.

Blending with your Spirit Guide(s):
For this example, let me show you how to ask Spirit about your life partnership.

Begin by asking Spirit the following:

1. When will I be with my life partner?

2. How will I know it is my life partner?

3. What can I do to make myself a best version of myself for my life partner?

4. What signs will I receive when my life partner is near?

5. Will we get married?

6. Will we have children?

Catch my drift? BLEND and go deeper with Spirit!

CREATING YOUR SPIRIT DICTIONARY
AND LANGUAGE WITH SPIRIT

The following is a blending exercise of Spirit Guides and deceased loved ones communicating their own language of messages for you:

1. Close your eyes and take six deep breaths.
2. Clear your mind by envisioning a "white board" or "chalk board."
3. Ask Spirit to show you images in your psychic mind (third eye – between your brows) to represent each of the following:
   - Symbols
   - Seasons
   - Numbers
   - Colors
   - Plants
   - Animals
   - Personality traits
   - Physical images & appearance
   - Songs
   - Phrases
   - Word associations
4. Ask Spirit to write their message or place your Spirit dictionary symbols and representations your psychic mind's "white board" or "chalk board."
5. Record it on the next page.

Record your messages and symbols here.

PRACTICING YOUR DICTIONARY DEVELOPMENT WITH SPIRIT

These are some easy to try exercises. Again, this will take you a long time to develop but with practice, these exercises below will give you a good head start!

Write the first thing that pops into your head using my 3 to 5 Second Rule. Don't overthink it. Don't wonder "who" is showing it to you. Just flow and remain out of ego.

1. Symbols (ex: guns if they were a hunter, cigars if they were a smoker, stylist scissors if they were a hair stylist, badge if they were an officer, etc.)

2. Seasons (ex: snow for winter, flowers for summer, Halloween decorations or pumpkins for October or fall, etc.)

3. Numbers or timing (Ex: a 5 is for May, or speak the month of June, show you numbers for birthdays, or times on a clock, etc.)

PSYCHIC MEDIUMSHIP EXERCISE

1. Sit in a quiet place without any external noise or distractions.

2. Take six deep breaths.

3. Calm and clear your mind.

4. Ask you Spirit Guides, "What is my next step in my life?"

Write all that you think, see and feel here. Try to be as detailed as possible.

REFLECTION EXERCISE

1. Has your intuition grown from the beginning of this workbook until now? If yes, write how and why. If no, write why.

2. Do you feel your Spirit Guides are around and that you are receiving signs? If yes, write how. If no, write why.

3. What was the most valuable lesson you learned on this new journey?

4. What have you learned to let go of?

5. What do you love about your ability to connect with your higher self and Spirit guidance?

6. What have you learned about yourself on this workbook journey?

7. How much time and practice you will I dedicate to your intuition, psychic abilities, and mediumship connection in your life?

SELF-EVALUATION

On a scale of 1 to 10 with 1 = the weakest and 10 = the strongest,

How would you rate trusting your intuition right now?

(look back at Chapter Seven for your previous answer)

Rating: _____

Write a heartfelt letter to your Spirit Guides and deceased loved ones expressing your gratitude to them for working alongside you on this workbook journey. Thank them for helping you to connect, grow, evolve, and unveil your own natural-born gifts and abilities.

Write a heartfelt letter to yourself complimenting and commending you for taking the time to awaken your spiritual self. Acknowledge all of the enlightenment, wisdom, knowledge, love, etc. you have found on this workbook journey.

ADDITIONAL NOTES:

MY HEARTFELT MESSAGE
&
MUAH PROJECT

Congratulations on getting this far! If you are reading this chapter, you have made incredible progress in unveiling your natural-born gifts of intuition, psychic abilities, and mediumship skills. I wish you a beautiful connection to the Spirit world the same way I have had for the last forty-five years.

I want to personally THANK YOU for choosing me as your psychic medium, spiritual teacher, author, and Doctor of Natural Health. I am humbled and honored that you chose me over so many other great spiritual mentors, teachers, and writers. I would love nothing more than my years of work and experience to become your vessel of connection to your higher self and Spirit guidance. I am grateful we were able to work together through this workbook and hope you truly enjoyed it. Allow the writing and exercises in this workbook to help guide you to the true authentic life you deserve. Enjoy this new journey, because from now on, it will be an incredible one. Please continue to put the inner work in; practice makes perfect!

You are an amazing badass soul who deserves all of the love, health, wealth, and abundance this life has to offer. Remember, your Universe is unlimited for your life through your channeling, manifesting, and connection.

For those who know me well, I refrained from swearing as much as possible throughout this book, LOL. That is because my workbook is meant to be used by ALL age groups, not just adults. If you feel this workbook can help resonate, relate, help, guide, and connect other people, perform a beautiful random act of humanity and purchase it as a gift and share with others.

With that said, in December of 2020, I was running errands on my day off when Spirit decided to give me a profound message. The vision Spirit showed me provided me the information, logo, name, and concept of what was to become the next chapter in my life. The information literally downloaded to my psychic mind like a movie reel. I will honestly tell you I didn't want to take anything else on at that moment in my life. I rebutted back to Spirit out loud as I was driving, "Right now I cannot take on another project!" Spirit responded, "That is okay, just start and it will morph." So, that is exactly what I did. I stopped running errands, went home, and immediately, began putting all Spirit showed me into action. With the help of my two incredible team members, Claudio and Michelle, we made this new project morph into my (our) reality. So, in January 2020, the Motherella's Unlimited Acts of Humanity community was birthed. Spirit's message allowed me to start my very own community of people who want to be a part of the best humanitarians in this lifetime. Though it is in its early stages, my goal is to build this community into mass numbers of people who want to give back to this world and become the gatekeepers of this beautiful planet; the way the Divine intended it to be.

You can follow and join our community at:

Motherella's Unlimited Acts of Humanity

MUAH Project

@muahproject on Facebook and Instagram

Logo design: Claudio Mendrano, Sannicola Media Productions.

Now, go be the badass you are meant to be!

Love, Motherella

ABOUT THE AUTHOR

Michelle Piper, known as "Motherella", is a gifted psychic medium with all six Claire's who has been channeling the Afterlife since she was six years old.

For over 13 years, Motherella has performed hundreds of thousands of readings for people around the world. She is raw, authentic, and her accuracy is mind-blowing. She gets rapid- fast messages from Spirit in paragraph form.

Motherella has an extensive background helping people connect to their Spirit Guides, Angels, and loves ones who have passed. She has helped countless people connect with their soul and find their life purpose. She has even assisted individuals in locating missing items. Motherella has also helped many people receive closure, peace, and healing from losing loved ones to unfortunate loss such as murder, overdose, suicide, and other tragic events. Under her guidance and mentoring, many psychic children have been able to understand and develop their psychic medium gifts.

As a Spiritual Teacher, she helps people with their mind, body, and soul alignment through Spirit and the Afterlife. Her passion is helping people shift their mindset, manifest their dreams, and connect with their soul and the Universe.

Michelle graduated Summa Cum Laude from the University of Natural Health and currently holds the following degrees and certifications:

Doctor of Philosophy in Holistic Natural Health & Nutrition
Doctor of Philosophy in Holistic Sports Nutrition
Board Certified-Midwife
Certified Natural Health Practitioner
Certified Holistic Nutrition Practitioner

In addition, she was awarded the following by the faculty of Ecclesiology in 2019:
Doctor of Divinity – Honorary Certificate
Ordained Holistic Natural Health & Healing Minister
Certified Spiritual Guide